Let America Decide

THE REPORT *of the* TWENTIETH CENTURY FUND TASK FORCE ON PRESIDENTIAL DEBATES

LET AMERICA DECIDE

With background paper by **Anthony Corrado**

1995 ◆ THE TWENTIETH CENTURY FUND PRESS ◆ NEW YORK

The Twentieth Century Fund sponsors and supervises timely analyses of economic policy, foreign affairs, and domestic political issues. Not-for-profit and nonpartisan, the Fund was founded in 1919 and endowed by Edward A. Filene.

Library of Congress Cataloging-in-Publication Data

Let America Decide: the report of the Twentieth Century Fund Task Force on Presidential Debates : with a background paper / by Anthony Corrado.
    p. cm.
    Includes index.
    ISBN 0-87078-381-5
    1. Presidents–United States–Election.   2. Presidents–United States–Election–1992.   3. Campaign debates–United States.   4. Television in politics–United States.   I. Corrado, Anthony.   1957–   .
II. Twentieth Century Fund.   Task Force on Presidential Debates.
JK524 .F33   1996   95–47694
324.7–dc20   CIP

Cover design and illustration: Claude Goodwin
Manufactured in the United States of America.

Foreword

In retrospect, the forces set in motion during the tumultuous decade of the 1960s are still at work reshaping much of American life. In politics, as in culture and family life, many of the most salient features of the 1990s can be best understood as the maturing of changes that first became apparent a generation ago.

Before the reforms of the 1960s took hold, for example, presidential primaries, although often of significance in the nominating process, were the method used for selecting only a small minority of delegates to national party conventions. Most delegates were chosen by local leaders and caucuses. State delegations were often tightly controlled by a few men (and they were all men) who weighed prospective candidates in terms of their electability and also bargained for the best deal for their regions. Today, such intermediaries have a place only among the cobwebs in the attic of our political history, along with daguerreotypes, whistle-stops, torchlight parades, and election day whiskey kegs. Now the prominence of "media gurus" and fund-raisers attests to the triumph of costly television advertising and dozens of primaries as the determining factors in the nominating process for the highest office in the land.

Of course, campaigns and governance both must adjust as technology and the nation evolve, but one factor stands out as common to almost everything that has happened to public life since the election of 1960: the emergence of television as the principal locus of public discourse in the United States. The Kennedy-Nixon debates have become the symbol of the nascent potency of television's effect on the election experience for voters.

The first debates were generally credited with providing the crucial margin of victory for John F. Kennedy in a very close election. But, despite their popularity, debates, like moon walks, were quickly abandoned. Sixteen years passed before the major candidates again met face to face on national television on the eve of an election. Since 1976, however, debates have been an expected and very important feature of presidential campaigns. Indeed, in view of the place they have played in recent political campaigns, it is surprising how close we came to having no debates in 1980 and again in 1992. These "close calls" are especially remarkable at a time when widespread unhappiness with the political process has prompted serious discussion of the dangers posed by a general lack of governmental legitimacy. Surely the nation would benefit from a high degree of confidence that presidential debates, something the public overwhelmingly desires, were a certain feature of the election process.

Legitimacy was very much on the minds of those at the Twentieth Century Fund and elsewhere who combined to help establish the Presidential Debate Commission before the 1988 election; the Twentieth Century Fund, in fact, was a sponsor of the conference at the Kennedy School in December 1986 that recommended establishing the Commission (replacing the sponsor of the earlier debates, the League of Women Voters), published the Report of the conference (*For Great Debates: A New Plan for Future Presidential TV Debates* by Newton N. Minow and Clifford M. Sloan), and then provided support for the formation of the Commission.

The Fund has long recognized the substantive and symbolic significance of the debates and the need for raising public awareness about issues relating to presidential politics. We have examined such diverse issues as the effects of television on presidential elections (*Presidential Television* by Newton N. Minow, John Bartlow Martin, and Lee M. Mitchell); the questions surrounding the need for debates (*Voters' Time: Report of the Twentieth Century Fund Commission on Campaign Costs in the Electronic Era; With the Nation Watching: Report of the Twentieth Century Fund Task Force on Televised Presidential Debates; Beyond Debate: A Paper on Televised Presidential Debates* by Joel L. Swerdlow; and *A Proper Institution: Guaranteeing Televised Presidential Debates* by John B. Anderson); and media coverage of presidential politics (*1-800-PRESIDENT: The Report of the Twentieth Century Fund Task Force on Television and the Campaign of 1992* and *The New News v. The Old News: The Press and Politics in the 1990s,* essays by Jay Rosen and Paul Taylor).

In 1992, a phenomenon that had played an important role in the 1980 debates, the emergence of a strong third-party candidate, along with changes in the format of debates raised novel and difficult issues for the Commission. Against this backdrop, the Trustees of the Fund, in 1993, decided that it was time to revisit this subject and authorized a new task force. While many of the issues discussed in the past are addressed in the pages that follow, the Task Force Report assumes one fundamental difference in the situation today: the concept of debates among the major presidential candidates has become deeply rooted in our politics. It seems quite unlikely that a major candidate would find it worthwhile to endure the opprobrium that accompanied a refusal to meet other challengers. But once the issue of whether or not debates will take place at all is off the table, questions about what kind of debates work best, what the public really wants, who should be included, and what the debates really accomplish are more significant than ever.

The Task Force also focused considerable attention on the existing Presidential Debate Commission. While one might imagine alternative institutional arrangements for organizing the debates themselves, the fact is that the Commission has actually functioned for the last two presidential campaigns and already has proposed a format for 1996. To be sure, in its present incarnation it has limits, and these are addressed in the Report of the Task Force. But the Task Force recognized the overwhelming practical benefit of the Commission's experience and legitimacy and recommended ways to strengthen its operations, rather than calling for an alternative mechanism.

The Task Force recognized that, at least given the current conventional wisdom, public preferences about what constitutes a "good" debate have shifted. The celebration of the so-called town meeting debate format in 1992 and the positive reaction to the single-moderator approach imply a basic rethinking of the role (if any) of journalists in the debates. In addition, in the age of instant polls and focus groups, the group discussed the trend toward using these devices more and more intrusively as part of debate coverage. There is a serious possibility, for example, that a network may tell us how a select group of people are reacting to the debate even as it is taking place. Would such a victory for technology be in the public interest?

Perhaps it is unavoidable, even preferable, that the future of debates will be shaped by technological and market changes in the media environment. The question then is will the debates live up to their potential for informing the public or will they increasingly become tailored-for-TV performances, where the quest for the most unorthodox question and the cleverest sound bite answer dominates the agenda? These questions are more than matters of taste for they go to the heart of the most important question of all: What should be done to maximize the chances that the debates will help to dampen skepticism and add legitimacy to the American political process?

These are not easy issues; nor do they lend themselves to a ready consensus for a diverse and thoughtful group such as the Task Force. But they are the right questions, and the debate about debates is richer because of the willingness of this group to take them on. No report about any aspect of our presidential campaigns can be a permanent blueprint for the future. American politics defies static analysis because it reflects the diversity and dynamism of the nation. Indeed, long-term prediction is especially perilous during this period of apparently fundamental transformation of public attitudes toward parties and government itself. Given these complexities, the thoughtful and comprehensive deliberations of this Task Force were impressive. On behalf of the Trustees of the Twentieth Century Fund, I thank them for their time and their contribution to this important subject.

RICHARD C. LEONE, PRESIDENT
The Twentieth Century Fund
November 1995

- Find topic for paper on presidency
- Go through papers for relevant information -
- Read for Presidency
  chapt 8
  p. 140-180 ?
- Read for Comparative Politics

- Find Sources for my annotated Bibliography.

University of Memphis

JK518 .B73 1986

Presidential campaigns

E176.1 M455 1992
Keith Melder

E183 .R96 1994
Running for pres.

Contents

Members of the Task Force

James F. Hoge, Jr., *Task Force Chair*
Editor, *Foreign Affairs*

John B. Anderson
Professor, Nova University Center for the Study of Law; former U.S. Representative from Illinois

Hodding Carter III
Knight Chair of Public Policy Journalism, University of Maryland

Michael Dukakis
Professor of Political Science, Northeastern University; former Governor of Massachusetts

Wyche Fowler, Jr.
Partner, Powell Goldstein Frazer and Murphy; former U.S. Senator from Georgia

Lawrence K. Grossman
President, Horizons Cable Network

Ellen Hume
Senior Fellow, Annenberg Washington Program

Kathleen Hall Jamieson
Dean and Professor of Communication, the Annenberg School for Communication, University of Pennsylvania

Bill Kovach
Curator, Nieman Foundation

Ellen Levine
Editor-in-Chief, *Good Housekeeping*

Dotty Lynch
Political Editor, CBS News

David A. Norcross
General Counsel, Republican National Committee

Carole Simpson
Anchorperson and Senior General Correspondent, ABC News

Ernest Tollerson
National Correspondent, *New York Times*

Ed Turner
Executive Vice President, CNN

Lowell Weicker
Chairman, Dresing-Leirman-Weicker; former Governor of Connecticut

Anne Wexler
Chairman, The Wexler Group

Thomas Winship
Chairman, The Center for Foreign Journalists

Anthony Corrado, *Task Force Executive Director and Background Paper Author*
Assistant Professor of Government, Colby College

EXECUTIVE SUMMARY

The 1992 presidential general election debates were a great improvement over those of the past decade. For the first time, both major-party nominees shared the stage with an independent candidate in a series of three-way debates. For the first time, the debates featured a variety of formats, including a town hall meeting forum in which citizens directly questioned those seeking the nation's highest office. These innovations helped generate substantial public interest. The 1992 debates were the most widely watched political event in American history, with an audience that grew larger with each debate. They focused public attention on the choice to be made on election day and dominated public discussion in the weeks leading up to the voting. Most important, they provided voters with valuable firsthand information, and after the election more people than ever before reported that they had relied on the debates in making their choice in the presidential balloting.

Yet, despite the ultimate success of the 1992 forums, few realize how close the nation came to not having debates or to having debates that did not include the independent candidate Ross Perot. Although the Commission on Presidential Debates announced a debate proposal well before the national party conventions, its efforts failed to discourage the candidates from engaging in the kinds of political posturing and lengthy debate about debates that had marred the planning of these events in the past. The Commission's plan was accepted by the Clinton campaign but was immediately rejected by the Bush campaign, which maintained that debates could only be determined through direct negotiations between the two campaigns. In contrast, the Clinton staff argued that the Commission should participate in any discussions. The two camps also argued over the number of debates to be held, where they should take place, and the formats to be used. These differences led to a prolonged period of disagreement between the candidates, which raised a very real possibility that debates might not be held at all.

This deadlock was finally broken less than six weeks before the election, when the representatives of the Bush and Clinton campaigns negotiated a debate agreement. They decided to include Ross Perot and his running mate, former admiral James Stockdale, in the debates, a stipulation to which the Commission had not yet consented. This forced the Commission to confront the issue of whether Perot should participate, an issue that was not resolved until the first week of October, less than a month before election day. Thus, a different 1992 outcome was only narrowly avoided. Had the major-party nominees disagreed on Perot's participation, there probably would have been no debates. Had the Commission decided not to include Perot, the current debates process would have been permanently undermined.

Given the 1992 experience and the rapid changes taking place in the national political environment, the Twentieth Century Fund decided that it was an appropriate time to convene a Task Force to assess the role of debates in presidential elections and to consider ways to improve them in the future. The Task Force, which met four times during 1995, was given a broad mandate to examine the major issues associated with these prestigious events. Our principal objective was to ensure substantive general election debates in the future. We believed that this goal would only be achieved by strengthening the Commission on Presidential Debates as an institution, by further improving the formats used in the debates, and by enhancing the quality of media coverage and public discussion accompanying the debates.

Among the Task Force's principal conclusions are the following:

- ◆ *The Commission on Presidential Debates should develop a more broadly based membership to reflect better the public's interest in the debates process.* As a beginning step, its membership should be expanded from the current ten members to twelve so that individuals who do not specifically represent the two major parties can be included. If the Commission is to retain its position as debate sponsor, it must have the confidence and respect of an increasingly cynical electorate. While we believe that party interests should be represented in the debates process, we also feel that the Commission should not be exposed to misperceptions or criticisms that may result from its bipartisan membership, because these charges may undermine its status.

One way to address this concern is to ensure that the Commission includes members who are perceived as representative of broader public interests than those of the two major parties. Such representation is especially important now since a significant proportion of the electorate is not committed to either major party and a strong possibility exists for a meaningful third or fourth candidate in a future presidential race.

♦ ***The Commission should adopt specific and public procedures for appointing members.*** In addition, the terms of members should be staggered, with each member appointed to a renewable four-year term with a limit of no more than two consecutive terms of service. Given its role in the presidential selection process, the Commission should operate with more openness and public accountability. Most of the public does not know who the Commission's members are, or how they are chosen. Nor do they know how its Advisory Board works, or how it is chosen. Most would be surprised to find out that the Commission is a self-perpetuating body with no provision for regular change in membership. Specific, well-publicized procedures that ensure a reasonable rotation in membership would enhance the Commission's institutional legitimacy and promote the incorporation of new perspectives and ideas in its decisionmaking.

♦ ***The Commission must continue to expand its public presence and civic education activities.*** The fundamental purpose of candidate debates is to promote a more informed citizenry. A debate sponsor therefore has an obligation to encourage public understanding of the debates process and engage in efforts that will make the debates more meaningful to voters. The Commission has undertaken a number of laudable civic education projects, but the efforts to date have been relatively limited in scope. The Task Force supports the Commission's current initiative to establish citizen debate-watch programs around the country and urges it to pursue additional means of promoting citizen education and participation in the process. In particular, the Commission should explore opportunities for building a debate component into existing voter education and outreach programs. It should also make all of its materials available through interactive formats so that they can receive as wide distribution as possible.

◆ *An endowment should be created for the Commission on Presidential Debates.* At present, the Commission relies on annual private contributions for its funding. A more stable financial base will increase its institutional strength and provide it with the resources needed to conduct more extensive public outreach and educational efforts. An endowment will reduce the Commission's dependence on sponsors who must be approached on a regular basis at a time when corporate and foundation resources face greater and greater pressures. It will also guard against the possibility of Commission members being distracted from other activities by fund-raising demands.

◆ *The purpose of general election debates is to provide the public with an opportunity to see the major candidates confront each other so that voters may learn more about the individuals who will be the next president and vice president of the United States.* The process must therefore ensure that the major candidates are invited to participate. Ross Perot's 1992 independent candidacy and the prospect of other significant non-major-party candidates in future elections led the Task Force to give serious consideration to the question of who should be invited to participate in the debates. The Commission has addressed this issue by developing a set of criteria designed to determine those candidates who have a "realistic" or "more than theoretical" chance of being elected the next president and vice president of the United States. The Task Force recognizes, however, the importance to the legitimacy of the process of guarding against the possibility of a candidate being excluded from the debates on the "realistic chance" criteria alone, even though that candidate enjoys substantial public support and is considered by many citizens to be worthy of inclusion in the debates. To avoid this possibility, the Commission should review its criteria to ensure that "any candidate with broad public support and a real likelihood of having a substantial impact on the outcome of the election" is invited to participate in the debates.

◆ *Debates best fulfill their purpose when conducted in a series employing different formats.* A series of varied debates offers candidates a better opportunity to make their cases to the electorate and places viewers in a better position to assess each candidate. At a minimum, there should be four presidential debates and one vice presidential debate prior to each election. At least one of the presidential debates should be held in early September to help stimulate public interest in the race and begin the process of focusing voters' attention on the choice they will face in November. As for the scheduling of the remaining debates, the Task Force favors continuing experimentation with the compacted, "miniseries" approach used in 1992, with the series scheduled in the final weeks of October. This approach ensures that debates are held when public interest in the campaign is reaching a peak and the people are most likely to watch.

♦ *Future debates should feature continued citizen participation and bolder, more innovative formats that stimulate interaction and actual debate between the candidates.* The Task Force was encouraged by the changes adopted in 1992 and feels that a town hall meeting debate or some other form of direct citizen participation should be included in future debates. But we also believe that even bolder innovations are necessary if debates are to fulfill their purpose of creating a more informed electorate. In particular, a direct candidate-to-candidate confrontation is long overdue. We therefore feel that at least one of the presidential debates should use a format that requires candidates to question each other directly and discuss what they consider the major issues in the race.

♦ *Debates are most effective when they are broadcast at times likely to attract a wide audience.* The Commission, networks, and candidates must work together to ensure that debates are given the highest priority and that they are broadcast in prominent prime-time slots. All of the parties involved in the process must be sensitive to the scheduling concerns raised in previous debates. In particular, the networks should give higher priority to these events and demonstrate a greater willingness to alter their regular programming so that debates can be broadcast when most people are likely to be watching. Broadcasters should also expand their efforts to promote debates and increase the number of public service announcements dedicated to them.

♦ ***Debate broadcasts should be expanded to include more networks and additional time slots.*** Given the expansion that has taken place in cable television, there is no reason why debate broadcasts should be limited to the evenings on which they take place or to networks that have traditionally covered them. The Task Force urges other networks to consider broadcasting or rebroadcasting the debates. By doing so, these networks will provide a larger share of the electorate with a chance to watch the debates and will create opportunities to see the debates more than once, which may further enhance their role in voter decisionmaking.

♦ ***Journalists should enhance their coverage of debates so that voters have the background information needed to make debates more meaningful.*** They should place less emphasis on polling and strategy and devote more attention to the substance of the debates. The Task Force concluded that current media coverage of the debates, which is dominated by polling analyses and the "horse race" aspects of these events, minimizes the educational value of the debates. We recognize that such horse race stories are inevitable, but we believe a much better job could be done in providing more balanced coverage. This is especially true in the days leading up to each debate since current reporting largely fails to provide voters with the contextual and substantive information needed to understand and assess better what they have heard in the debates. By improving the quality of debate coverage, journalists can help encourage critical thinking and independent judgment on the part of the electorate.

The information and positions discussed by the Task Force before reaching its conclusions, as well as other specific recommendations for reforming the debates process, are provided in the text of the Report.

REPORT OF THE TASK FORCE

None of the recent developments in political communication has made as valuable a contribution to the electoral process as the advent of presidential candidate debates. While the rapid expansion of cable television, talk radio programs, satellite transmission technologies, and the information superhighway have provided candidates with unprecedented means of communicating with the electorate, most of what passes as political information still consists of thirty-second campaign ads, brief sound bites on news broadcasts, and campaign-staged photo opportunities. Only debates allow voters to compare and analyze the major candidates in a common setting, answering the same questions and responding to each other in an immediate and direct manner. They also offer viewers a chance to assess the candidates without the mediating influence of the press or campaign spokespersons. Debates thus focus voters' attention on the choices they will face in an election and encourage independent judgments. They stimulate the type of informed decisionmaking that is essential in deciding who will best represent the nation.

Debates also constitute the only opportunity during the course of a general election campaign in which the major contenders for our nation's highest office appear together and directly present their views to a nationwide audience. They provide candidates with a unique forum to explain their reasons for seeking the presidency, articulate their views on the problems facing the nation, and set forth the policies they hope to pursue if elected to serve in office. They encourage candidates to acknowledge their responsibility to the citizenry and enhance the public's capacity to hold candidates accountable for their views. At the same time, debates reinforce the tradition of open political discussion that is a cornerstone of democratic government.

Most observers agree that the 1992 debates were a great improvement over those of the past decade and may prove to be a watershed in the history of these events. For the first time, the major-party nominees shared the stage with an independent candidate in a series of three-way debates. For the first time, the debates featured a variety of formats, including a highly innovative town hall meeting forum in which undecided voters questioned the candidates. More debates were held—three presidential and one vice presidential—than in any of the elections in the 1980s. And, most important, the debates drew large audiences and substantial public interest. In fact, they were cumulatively the most widely watched political event in history, with each subsequent presidential debate drawing a larger audience than the previous meeting for the first time ever.

Yet, as in the past, the debates were surrounded by controversy. Few realize how close the nation came to not having debates or to having debates that did not include Ross Perot. The planning of these forums was marred by political posturing, a lengthy "debate over debates," and conflicts over format and candidate control. While the Clinton campaign readily accepted the proposed debate plan advanced by the Commission on Presidential Debates, the Bush campaign refused to consider it, demanding instead that the candidates negotiate an agreement on their own. The Bush campaign's position led to a prolonged period of disagreement between the candidates, which raised a very real possibility that debates might not be held at all. This deadlock was finally broken in the last week of September. But before a final decision was reached, Ross Perot reentered the race, forcing the Commission to confront the issues involved in deciding whether the independent candidate should be invited to participate. As a result, a debate agreement sanctioned by all participants was not completed until the first week of October, less than a month before election day.

The 1992 experience thus raised a host of issues regarding the debates process and the future of general election debates. Can the current process guarantee that debates will be a central feature of presidential campaigns in the future? Is the Commission on Presidential Debates an effective debate sponsor? How can the type of candidate machinations and disputes that have plagued the process in recent elections be avoided? How can the natural bargaining advantage of front-runners and incumbents be offset? Were the new formats used in the 1992 debates successful? Did they best suit the informational needs of the electorate? Finally, is the current process flexible and adaptive enough to accommodate the broad changes taking place in national politics and the new forms of political communication?

Given these issues and the rapid changes taking place in the national political environment, the Twentieth Century Fund decided that it was an appropriate time to convene a Task Force to assess the experience with debates in presidential elections and to consider their role in the future. The Task Force, which met four times during 1995, was given a broad mandate to examine the major issues associated with presidential debates. To a certain extent we viewed our efforts as building on the work of previous Twentieth Century Fund task forces on presidential debates and political communication. Yet, while we did revisit some old and enduring problems, our primary goal was to take a fresh look at debates with an eye toward making recommendations that would not only address current matters, but also look ahead to some of the issues that may become prevailing concerns in the near future.

We recognized that our deliberations were taking place in a period of dramatic change and flux in national politics. Public dissatisfaction with the political system remains high, as does the percentage of voters demanding change in the conduct of political campaigns. A sizable percentage of voters no longer affiliate themselves with either of the two major parties, and in recent elections significant numbers of citizens have opted to break from traditional voting patterns and consider new alternatives. Many others have become so dissatisfied with and alienated from the system that they have decided not to participate at all. As a result, the prospects for independent or alternative party candidacies are on the rise, increasing the possibility that future presidential campaigns will be contested by more than just the nominees of the two major parties. If the debates are to continue to play a major role in voter decisionmaking, debate sponsors will have to be prepared for new possibilities and the process must be flexible enough to accommodate changing political circumstances.

We also realize that significant changes are taking place in the ways campaigns are conducted. In an effort to meet the public outcry for a more responsive political system, candidates have demonstrated a surprising willingness to pursue new forms of communications and new techniques to reach out to their constituents. These shifting attitudes, combined with the growth in new technologies available to candidates, make it difficult to predict exactly what will happen in the future. Who, for example, would have predicted the extensive use of daytime talk shows or infomercials in the 1992 election? Or the use of a town hall meeting format in the presidential debates?

Who knows what effects the availability of the Internet and its vast communication capacities will have on the conduct of the 1996 campaign? Or how willing the candidates may be to debate each other in traditional or nontraditional formats and venues?

Yet, even in acknowledging these changes, the Task Force believed that debates will continue to play a vital role in presidential campaigns for the foreseeable future. The Task Force thus began its deliberations by considering whether additional steps should be taken to guarantee debates in the future. The public has demonstrated a deep interest in debates; these are the events in a presidential campaign they care most about and to which they pay the most attention. Voters have come to expect debates and consider them a crucial component of the presidential campaign. Thus, one method of helping to promote public confidence in the electoral process and perceptions of responsiveness in the political system is to guarantee that this expectation is fulfilled.

THE COMMISSION ON PRESIDENTIAL DEBATES

One important step toward guaranteeing debates in the future is to institutionalize and strengthen the legitimacy of the current debates process. For the past two elections, the debates have been sponsored by the Commission on Presidential Debates, a private, nonprofit organization whose sole purpose is to organize, manage, produce, publicize, and support presidential candidate debates. The Commission was established in 1987, partly in response to a study supported by the Twentieth Century Fund, by the chairs of the Republican and Democratic National Committees to serve as an independent debate sponsor funded solely by private contributions. The Commission was created because it was thought to have the most likely prospect of carrying out this important task. It would have more influence on nominees than the League of Women Voters, which had previously sponsored the debates, and would be more independent than the television networks or major political parties.

The Task Force carefully reviewed the activities of the Commission and agreed that it had fulfilled the obligations of a debate sponsor well. It has stood as an advocate of the public interest in a complicated process that is rife with partisan concerns. It has efficiently carried out the myriad of tasks that are essential to staging the debates, including early negotiations with networks regarding formats and schedules, the selection of potential sites, and the production of the telecasts. Its efforts to advance proposals early in the election year have helped to promote public dialogue about the debates and initiate candidate discussions. It has also sponsored a number of studies and postelection symposiums that have significantly improved our knowledge of the effects of debates and their role in voter decisionmaking.

The rationale behind the creation of the Commission remains a sound one. Such an organization is an appropriate locus for the management of these events. But we also feel that the Commission is still too frail an instrument. Its authority stemmed from its independent and bipartisan status, as well as from public perceptions of its legitimacy as the sponsor of general election debates. In 1988 and 1992, this authority was challenged by both prospective sponsors and the Bush campaign. In 1988, the League of Women Voters opposed the creation of the Commission and refused to share sponsorship responsibilities with the organization, thus ending the League's role as a sponsor of general election debates. In both 1988 and 1992, the Bush campaign took the position that the Commission should not be granted a special sponsorship status and refused to negotiate directly with Commission members. The Commission's ability to withstand these challenges is a testament to its integrity and durability, and indicates the extent to which it has already established itself as a political institution. But this does not guarantee that it will be able to withstand similar or more severe challenges in the future.

If the Commission is to retain its position, it must have the confidence and respect of an increasingly cynical electorate. It must also become stronger as an institution, so that candidates will not risk defying its authority. And it must operate with more openness and public accountability. Most of the public does not know who the Commission's members are, or how they are chosen. Nor do they know how its Advisory Board works, or how it is chosen. Accordingly, the Task Force considered how best to strengthen the Commission's public presence and solidify its status as debate sponsor.

REFORM THE STRUCTURE AND APPOINTMENTS PROCESS

The Commission has cast itself as a *non*partisan debate sponsor, but it is firmly rooted in the two major parties. Although independent of the national party organizations, it was created and is now cochaired by the former heads of the Democratic and Republican National Committees. Moreover, its other eight members have always been individuals clearly associated with either of the two major parties. There is no bloc of "independent" members to reinforce the fairness of its decisionmaking. Consequently, many observers perceive the Commission not as nonpartisan but as a *bi*partisan institution that primarily represents the interests of the major parties.

Further steps need to be taken to ensure that the Commission acts in a nonpartisan manner. While we believe that individuals with partisan affiliations should be included on the Commission and that party interests should be represented in the debates process, the Commission's work should not be exposed to misperceptions or criticisms about its partisan bias that may undermine its status. One way to address this concern is to ensure that the Commission includes members who are perceived as representative of broader public interests rather than particular major-party interests. Such representation is especially important now since a significant minority of the electorate is not committed to either major party and a strong possibility exists for a meaningful third or fourth candidate in a future presidential race.

We therefore recommend that the Commission work to develop a more broadly based membership to reflect better the public's interest in the debates process. As a beginning step, its membership should be expanded from the current ten members to twelve so that individuals who do not specifically represent the two major parties can be included. These additional members should be recognized figures in public affairs and might include former public servants, educational or political leaders, prominent businesspersons, or public interest advocates.

We further recommend that the Commission adopt specific and public procedures for appointing members and setting terms of service. At present, there are no limits on the terms of commissioners, and the Commission itself appoints new members when a vacancy opens. In other words, under current practice the Commission is a self-perpetuating body. Although the Commission has experienced substantial turnover in recent years (half of the original members have been replaced over the past five years), such change is by no means mandatory. *We believe that the Commission should appoint a nominating committee from among the members of its forty-person Advisory Board.* This committee would be responsible for suggesting new appointees when vacancies occur, with these nominees subject to Commission approval. *In addition, the terms of members should be staggered, with each member appointed to a renewable four-year term with a limit of no more than two consecutive terms of service.* This will ensure a reasonable rotation in membership, which will help to promote the incorporation of new perspectives and ideas into Commission decisionmaking.

EXPAND PUBLIC EDUCATION ACTIVITIES

We also recommend that the Commission continue to expand its public presence. While the debates have captured the public's attention, many citizens do not fully understand the debates process and are not aware of the Commission's activities. The Task Force believes that heightened public awareness of the Commission and its role will further strengthen its institutional legitimacy. This end can be achieved in large part by continuing to expand the Commission's civic education activities.

Since the fundamental purpose of candidate debates is to promote a more informed citizenry, a sponsoring organization has an obligation to encourage public knowledge of the process and engage in efforts that will make the debates more meaningful to voters. The Commission has undertaken a number of laudable civic education projects, such as producing and distributing promotional and educational materials, staging a quadrennial public conference, and sponsoring focus group and other research activities to gauge public response and determine the effects of debates. But efforts to date have been relatively limited in scope.

The Commission has already begun to extend its activities in the 1996 election cycle by taking the lead in planning debate-watch programs throughout the nation, where groups of citizens will gather in various locations to view the debates and discuss them with the assistance of trained moderators. We endorse this effort and encourage organizations such as the National Association of Broadcasters, League of Women Voters, local media organizations, and the academic community to participate in this program.

We also urge the Commission to pursue additional means of promoting citizen education and participation in the process. Such measures should not be limited to presidential election years, but should be carried out on an ongoing basis throughout the course of each presidential election cycle. *In particular, we recommend the development of curricular materials that can be used in schools throughout the nation to educate students about the role of debates and encourage them to watch these events. A debate guidebook should also be produced that includes information on such topics as the history of the debates, the role of the Commission, the schedule of events, formats, and background on the candidates. The Commission should also explore opportunities for building a debate component into existing voter education and outreach programs. All of these materials should receive as wide a distribution as possible.*

In addition, we believe the Commission should make all of its materials available to the public through interactive formats. The Commission has already taken an important first step toward this end by establishing a World Wide Web site on the Internet that promotes its works, makes available recent press releases and official statements, and provides background material on the citizen debate-watch project. *The Commission's World Wide Web site should be expanded to include background information on the presidential debates process, an indexed transcript of each of the presidential and vice presidential debates, and transcripts of its postelection conferences and research reports. This would ensure that official transcripts and the findings of such materials as the Commission's focus group studies would be available to a wide audience.*

ESTABLISH AN ENDOWMENT

Another essential aspect of institutional strength is a stable financial base. The Commission's operations are currently financed through the private contributions it solicits. The funding for operating revenues comes primarily from contributions received from corporate donors and foundation sources. This funding is not guaranteed; each year the Commission must solicit the money it needs to continue its work. The costs of producing the debates, which are approximately $500,000 per debate, are raised through donations generated by the host sites (which are usually academic settings in line with the educational purpose of the debates) or host cities. To date, the Commission has not encountered major difficulties in generating the revenues needed to produce the debates; indeed, in each election cycle many cities and academic institutions have eagerly offered to serve as potential hosts due to the prestige of these events. In 1992, however, the lack of a debate agreement until early October and the close scheduling of the actual debates created a very short timetable that made fund-raising problematic. Commission staff had to spend a substantial amount of time raising the funds needed to produce the debates and meet the additional expenses generated by the compact schedule.

A stronger financial base will make the Commission less dependent on annual revenues. It will free the organization from a need to rely on sponsors who must be approached on a yearly basis at a time when corporate and foundation resources face greater and greater pressures. It will also lessen the need to depend on the largesse of host cities, as well as guard against the possibility of Commission members being distracted from other activities by fund-raising demands. Most important, an improved financial base will provide the Commission with the staff and resources needed to conduct the more extensive public outreach and educational efforts that we have called for.

The Task Force strongly believes that an endowment should be established for the Commission on Presidential Debates. We urge the Twentieth Century Fund to take the lead in working with the Commission to recruit the support of other foundations and donors to build such an endowment. This endowment should ultimately be large enough to reduce significantly the Commission's dependence on private gifts for its annual operating revenues.

CANDIDATE PARTICIPATION

The purpose of general election debates is to provide the public with an opportunity to see the major candidates confront each other, so that voters can gain the information needed to help make a final choice about whom to support. The process must therefore ensure that the major candidates are included in the debates. But this is not as simple as it may appear; in fact, the question of candidate participation has proved to be one of the thornier issues in the debates process.

While the candidate selection process must be inclusive, it must not be so open that it diminishes the value of these forums in helping individuals obtain the information they need to make a final choice. To include individuals who are not viable challengers for the Oval Office would undermine the voters' ability to focus sharply on the major candidates and minimize the time available to the major candidates to share their views with the electorate. The inclusion of nonviable candidates would therefore reduce the educational value of the debates and might also erode public perceptions of the legitimacy of the debates process. It would also risk nonparticipation by the major-party candidates. It would certainly not enhance the civic benefits of the debates.

Selecting debate participants is complicated by the wide pool of announced candidates. Although the two major-party nominees are the focal point of public attention in a presidential election, a sizable number of individuals register as candidates for the office. In 1992, for example, more than 125 persons registered with the Federal Election Commission as presidential candidates, and dozens more announced that they were seeking the office. Such a large number is not atypical.

The debates process therefore requires a set of reasonable criteria for deciding who should be allowed to participate. The Commission on Presidential Debates has sought to meet this need and ensure an open and fair selection process by developing a broad set of nonpartisan criteria for determining debate participation. These criteria, which were developed by members of the Commission's Advisory Board prior to the 1988 election and slightly revised prior to 1992, are designed to identify those candidates who have, if not a realistic, then at least a "more than theoretical" chance of being elected the next president or vice president of the United States. The criteria are very comprehensive and move far beyond the measures used in previous elections; in addition to polling data, they include assessments of a candidate's national organization, other measures of public support, and determinations of a candidate's "newsworthiness and competitiveness."

The Commission has now used its selection criteria in two elections without major controversy. In 1988, the Commission reviewed a number of candidates and decided to invite only the major-party nominees to participate in the general election forums. In 1992, the guidelines were used to judge whether Perot and a number of others should be included in the debates; only Perot and the major-party nominees were deemed to have met the criteria. The way the process works is that the Commission's Advisory Board reviews potential participants to determine whether they fulfill the criteria and then makes a recommendation to the Commission. In reaching its conclusion, the Advisory Board solicits the views of news editors, political scientists, and other close observers in order to ensure a fully informed and fair decision. A final decision is then up to the Commission, which can either accept or reject the Board's recommendation.

In implementing its criteria, the Advisory Board has adopted the operative principle that the purpose of the debates is to enable the electorate to confront a final choice of which candidates to support for our nation's highest offices. In the Board's view, the purpose of general election debates is not to introduce candidates to the electorate or provide minor candidates with a forum for having their views heard. Instead, it is to present to the electorate the individuals likely to win the election, one of whom will be the next president of the United States.

We agreed that the Commission has done an admirable job of balancing competing claims and devising guidelines that ensure the participation of major candidates without opening the floodgates to include four or five or more candidates in the debates. The Commission's criteria represent a major improvement over past efforts. They guarantee that a broad range of factors and a representative range of opinions are brought to bear on the assessment of individual candidacies. Most important, they ensure a fair and timely assessment of non-major-party candidates.

Moreover, we shared the Commission's view that the purpose of general election debates is to give voters a chance to learn more about the individuals who will be the next president and vice president. These debates must encourage the electorate to consider the meaningful choice it will face on election day. To do otherwise would undermine the purpose of these forums and do little to promote the public interest.

The role of general election debates is not to introduce the electorate to every choice available or to provide all non-major-party candidates with a free forum for making their views known to a larger, nationwide audience. We do not believe that candidates who lack significant public support, or even those who enjoy the support of 3 or 4 percent of the electorate in a close two-party race, should be included.

Nor do we believe that non-major-party candidates must participate in the debates in order to gain public attention. Independent and minor-party candidates now have many more opportunities to share their views with the electorate than they have had in the past. The growth of cable television, radio and television talk shows, and public affairs programs, as well as the information superhighway, offer independent and minor-party candidates a wide array of vehicles for making their views known to an increasingly large proportion of the electorate. While these vehicles do not enjoy the prestige or audience of a presidential debate, they offer candidates reasonable opportunities to build the support needed to meet the Commission's criteria.

We recognize, however, that it is important to the legitimacy of the process to guard against the possibility that a candidate who enjoys substantial public support, and who many citizens feel should be included in the debates, is excluded on the "realistic chance" criteria alone. Many Task Force members questioned whether the Commission's current approach might exclude candidates who could have "a substantial impact on the outcome of an election" but do not have a "realistic chance" of winning the race. For example, would the current criteria guarantee inclusion of a candidate who generated substantial public interest but was not projected to win a significant number of electoral college votes—or any electoral college votes—as ultimately proved to be the case with Perot?

To avoid this possibility, the Commission should be willing to ensure that a candidate with broad support and a real likelihood of having a substantial impact on the outcome of an election is invited to participate in the debates. We believe that this objective can be achieved within the framework of the current selection criteria, so long as the Commission continues to exercise good judgment in its decisions and is willing to exercise flexibility in the implementation of its guidelines.

FORMATS

The rules of debate, topics, the questions and questioners, and other factors that constitute format should be designed to engage the public's attention and provide viewers with as much information as possible about the candidates and their positions. In this regard, the 1992 debates represented a substantial improvement over those of previous elections. Prior to 1992, most presidential debates featured a press panel format in which a number of journalists posed questions to the candidates. This format was widely criticized as uninteresting to viewers and of lesser value to voters than other approaches due to the proclivity of the panelists to ask hypothetical or provocative questions that were often only tangentially related to the electorate's primary concerns. Although suggestions for improving the format were made throughout the 1980s, few of these were adopted by the candidates. As a result, in each subsequent election, criticism of the format increased, which led the Commission on Presidential Debates to recommend replacement of the press panel with a single-moderator format for all of the proposed 1992 debates. Although the 1992 forums did not strictly follow the Commission's plan, they did dramatically depart from the press panel formula. In fact, each debate featured a different format: the first presidential debate used a traditional press panel, the second a very innovative town hall meeting approach, and the third a combination of a single-moderator and a press panel. The vice presidential debate used a single-moderator format.

The Task Force supports the idea of a series of debates employing different formats. This approach allows voters to see the candidates confront each other in different settings. For the public, this provides an opportunity to gain an extensive amount of firsthand information about the candidates over a period of time. For the candidates, it guards against the prospect of being judged solely on the basis of a single forum or a particular format. A series of varied debates thus offers the candidates a better opportunity to make their case to the electorate and places viewers in a better position to assess meaningfully each candidate's intelligence and character.

The best way to maximize the information available to voters is to have an ample number of debates. *At a minimum, there should be four presidential debates and one vice presidential debate prior to each election. At least one of the presidential debates should be held in early September to help stimulate public interest in the race and begin the process of focusing voters' attention on the choice they will face in November. As for the scheduling of the remaining debates, the Task Force favored continued experimentation with the compacted, "miniseries" approach used in 1992, with the series scheduled in the final weeks of October.* This approach ensures that debates are held when public interest in the campaign is reaching a peak and people are most likely to watch. A compact schedule may also enhance the value of the debates since it provides viewers with a substantial amount of information in a relatively short period of time.

The Task Force chose not to recommend a rigid format structure or design for the 1996 debates and beyond. We were encouraged by the adaptation and flexibility demonstrated in the 1992 process. We hope that in the future debate planners will continue to experiment with formats and schedules in an effort to produce meaningful debates that best meet the needs of changing political circumstances. We especially encourage the Commission to pursue formats that will stimulate more direct and spontaneous exchanges among the participants. We did, however, discuss the relative merits of different formats and offer

a number of suggestions that we believe should serve as guidelines for
the development of future debates.

CITIZEN PARTICIPATION

The most notable innovation in the 1992 debates was the adoption of
the town hall meeting format for the second presidential debate,
which was held in Richmond, Virginia. In this forum, a selected group
of citizens questioned the candidates directly with the guidance of a
single moderator. The participants were all undecided voters from
the Richmond area who were chosen on the basis of a scientific selection process conducted by the Gallup organization. Neither the candidates nor the moderator had any knowledge of the questions
beforehand.

The Task Force was especially enthusiastic about this debate.
This format stimulated public interest and demonstrated the ability of
individual citizens to ask relevant questions of the candidates when
given an opportunity to do so. *We therefore concluded that a town
hall meeting debate or some other format that incorporates direct
citizen participation should be a central feature of future debates.*
Giving citizens a meaningful role in such an important event high-
lights the responsiveness of the system to voter concerns, which in
turn helps to legitimize the process. It also reinforces one of the most
fundamental principles of our electoral system: that candidates are
accountable to the public for their views.

While we endorse the notion of direct citizen participation, the
Task Force cautions that care must be exercised in the selection of
participants. Experience with the town hall meeting format in recent
U.S. Senate and House elections has demonstrated one potential
drawback of this approach: the audience recruited to question the
candidates may include many representatives of partisan organizations or interest groups whose questions reflect a narrow agenda. To
guard against this possibility at the presidential level, we recommend
that scientifically based, random sampling procedures conducted by
a well-respected, independent polling organization, similar to those
employed by the Commission on Presidential Debates in 1992, be
used to select all individuals invited to take part in any debate that
includes a direct citizen participation component.

*The Commission should continue to explore other means
of involving the citizenry in the debates process.* In this regard, we

believe the Commission's efforts to encourage the formation of
debate-watch programs that will promote public dialogue about the
debates and provide citizens with opportunities to share their views
with each other to be a valuable addition to the overall debates process. These efforts, however, should be expanded to take advantage of
the new communications technologies that are rapidly emerging. In
particular, we urge the Commission to begin to explore how new
interactive communications approaches can be used to involve citizens further in the general election debates.

PRESS PANELS

The use of the press panel format has proved to be one of the most
controversial aspects of presidential debates. Critics have long argued
that this format essentially turns the debates into glorified press conferences that tend to diminish the amount of confrontation and clash
between the candidates. They also note that this approach reduces the
amount of speaking time available to the candidates and often pro-
duces questions that are not directly relevant to voters' major concerns. Accordingly, they conclude that this format does not best serve
the informational needs of the electorate.

In 1992, debate planners sought to address these criticisms by
moving away from the press panel format. The Commission on
Presidential Debates' preliminary proposal for these forums sought
to replace the traditional press panel with a single moderator for all
four debates. The final plan agreed to by the candidates and approved
by the Commission called for the use of the press panel in only the first
presidential debate and the last part of the final presidential debate.

One issue raised by the 1992 experience is whether the press
panel format should be used in future debates. Some Task Force
members expressed the view that press panels can continue to serve
a valuable role. These members noted that a panel of journalists who
have covered the campaign tends to be more familiar with the particular issues associated with specific policy proposals than an individual moderator or a group of citizens. They further observed that
journalists are in a better position to highlight conflicting statements
or positions that might have emerged during the course of the campaign. Most Task Force members, however, shared the concerns
raised by critics of the press panel format. These members generally
argued that press panels should be replaced by a single-moderator format

or some other approach that gives the candidates more time to express their views and reduces the role of journalists in the debates process.

The Task Force agreed that the press panel approach should no longer stand as the primary model for presidential debates. Instead, most members believed that the debates should rely on a single moderator and employ more innovative formats that would increase the amount of dialogue and interaction among the participants.

The Task Force further concluded that if a press panel is used in a future debate, two changes in procedure are necessary. First, in no instance should the candidates be granted a right of approval with respect to the participating journalists. Allowing candidates a role in selecting panelists places the candidates' own interests before the public interest and does not improve the quality of the debates. Moreover, it undermines public perception of the legitimacy and fairness of the debates process. We strongly believe that the Commission on Presidential Debates should be solely responsible for choosing participants. *Second, we feel that panelists should be able to ask follow-up questions.* In recent elections, candidates have often refused to allow this practice. We feel that this restriction serves neither the candidates' nor the voters' interests. Follow-up questions present an opportunity to solicit additional information or clarify a candidate's response and thus can be of great benefit to those watching a debate. They also offer candidates the chance to explain their positions more fully and clarify the ways their thinking differs from that of an opponent. Consequently, we recommend that follow-up questions be permitted in every debate.

FUTURE INNOVATIONS

While we support the format changes adopted in 1992, we are convinced that even bolder innovations should be considered for the future to make the debates a more valuable tool for civic education. We do not, however, support changes solely designed to make the debates more visually interesting or entertaining to audiences. The measure of a debate is the quality of information and understanding it offers the viewer. Any future changes in format should therefore be assessed on the basis of the effect they may have in terms of encouraging voters to watch substantive debates.

One way to stimulate viewer interest and more informative debates is to enhance the amount of interaction and actual *debate* between the candidates. *We therefore recommend that at least one of the presidential debates use a format that allows the candidates to address each other directly and engage in a dialogue on what they regard as the major issues in the campaign.* The time has come for a debate at the presidential level in which the candidates ask questions of each other and undertake a conversation, with a moderator present solely to perform the task of keeping the discussion moving along. This format has been used successfully in a number of nonpresidential debates. It would provide the citizenry with a unique opportunity to see the candidates confront each other and defend their views in an unmediated way.

Another alternative that should be tried is the "Lincoln-Douglas" style debate, or a debate in which candidates are asked to address a particular topic and given longer periods to respond to questions. This type of debate would be best suited to an election in which there is a prominent or compelling national issue that stands as the primary concern of most voters. This format would offer voters a relatively substantial amount of information on the major issue in the race, instead of information on diverse subjects designed to provide viewers with an overall perspective on a candidate. This latter purpose, however, would be served by the other debates conducted over the course of the general election campaign.

MANDATING DEBATES

Another innovation that legislators and political observers have discussed in recent years is the adoption of federal legislation that would require candidates to participate in debates as a condition of accepting public funding. The Task Force considered whether a legislative solution of this type is needed and whether it would improve the process. We concluded that such a law should not be adopted.

Many members felt that the public's desire to see the candidates debate is now strong enough to ensure that these forums would continue to be held in the future. A candidate who is perceived as trying to avoid debates faces substantial public pressure to participate, as evidenced by the public response to Bush's delaying tactics in 1992. Such a candidate also runs a high risk of losing public support. Public demands and political realities have thus reached a point where they constitute significant inducements to encourage candidates to debate.

Other members, however, noted that the negotiations between the candidates came perilously close to breaking down in both 1988 and 1992, and that elections without debates were narrowly avoided. Some of those members therefore argued that candidates who accept public financing in the general election campaign should be required to participate in debates as a condition of such funding. They observed that candidates should participate in debates as a matter of civic obligation, and that a requirement to appear in three or four debates is a relatively minor condition when compared to the tens of millions of dollars in taxpayers' money these candidates receive from the Presidential Election Campaign Fund.

A majority of the Task Force concluded that legislation mandating debate participation, or any other effort to require participation by tying it to public funding or some other mechanism, should not be recommended at this time. A number of individuals expressed the view that such a requirement would amount to coercion. The tens of millions of dollars in public financing are so essential to a presidential campaign that no candidate would be likely to forgo this resource in exchange for having to participate in the debates. That raises serious constitutional issues, especially with respect to First Amendment protections and the right of a candidate to choose not to debate. It might also lead to further legislative interference in the process or micromanagement of the debates, which could result in a loss of the flexibility and innovation demonstrated in the 1992 cycle.

THE ROLE OF THE MEDIA

Debates best fulfill their function in a democratic society when they are viewed by a wide audience and serve as a stimulus for a broader public discussion of the issues and candidates in a race. Accordingly, one of the principal goals of the debates process must be to maximize the viewership of these events. Yet, once again in 1992, debate planners failed to reach an agreement with network broadcasters that would achieve this goal. The candidates did not reach an agreement with each other until the end of September, well after fall network schedules had been set. Some of the major networks displayed resistance to the idea of holding debates on evenings when popular programs or major sporting events were scheduled to be aired. They also sought to have the debates aired early in the evening to reduce their effect on prime-time programming, which made viewing inconvenient for citizens on the West Coast. Such problems are not new. In the past, CBS failed to broadcast a presidential debate because it conflicted with a major league baseball playoff game, while NBC joined a debate in progress rather than interrupt a football game that had not yet finished.

ENCOURAGE DEBATE VIEWERSHIP

We contend that debates are most effective when they are broadcast at times most likely to attract a wide audience. All of the parties involved in the debates process should therefore be sensitive to the scheduling concerns raised in previous debates. The Commission on Presidential Debates, the networks, and the candidates must work together more closely to ensure that debates are broadcast when viewership is likely to be at a peak. Most important, it is necessary for candidates to negotiate arrangements much earlier in the campaign and consult the Commission and the networks, so that a proper schedule can be arranged. This will help avoid the sort of scheduling changes and uncertainties that occurred in 1992 as a result of the candidates' failure to arrive at an agreement until late in the campaign.

The networks should work with the Commission to make sure that prime-time broadcast slots are available, including Sunday evenings and midweek nights. They should also give greater priority to the debates and demonstrate a greater willingness to alter their regular programming or delay the broadcast of sports events for the sake of the debates. Since the debates are held only once every four years, we do not believe that it is unfair or overly burdensome to ask the networks to make the best times available for these important civic events.

Besides expanding the availability of prime-time slots, broadcasters should also expand their efforts to promote them. Specifically, the networks should increase the number of public service announcements (PSAs) aired to promote these events. These PSAs, which should emphasize the time and date of each forum, should be concentrated in the days leading up to each debate and aired during prime-time viewing hours. Such announcements will help ensure the maximum possible audience for the debates.

We also strongly recommend that broadcast of the debates be expanded to include more networks and additional time slots. We urge other networks, such as MTV, the History Channel, the Discovery

Channel, and the Family Channel, to consider broadcasting or rebroadcasting the debates. By airing the debates at additional times, these networks will not only provide a larger share of the electorate with a chance to watch the debates, but they will also create opportunities for those in the electorate who are interested in doing so to see the debates more than once, which may further enhance the role of these events in voter decisionmaking.

Improve Debate Coverage

Most observers of the presidential debates process have been critical of the media coverage surrounding these events. The most common criticism is that journalists devote too much attention to the strategic dimensions of the debates, focusing on the candidates' respective tactics, the horse race aspects of these forums, and the determination of who "won" and "lost" each debate. A majority of the Task Force shared this view and noted that such coverage minimizes the educational value of the debates. Instead of helping voters understand the issues in the race and the differences in the candidates' positions, this type of coverage emphasizes performance over substance and polling numbers over policy proposals. It encourages voters to see the debates as part of a broader strategic game and to focus on misstatements or "gaffes" rather than substantive differences between the candidates and the feasibility of their proposals. Such coverage also tends to promote collective decisions about the outcome of each debate based on instant survey results, rather than the sort of individualized decisionmaking that leads to a well-informed vote.

We believe that journalists need to devote more attention to the substance of the debates. In particular, journalists and media organizations should place greater emphasis on the task of providing voters with the background information they need to better understand the contents of a debate. For example, in the days preceding each debate, news reports should offer more stories that recap the race to date and offer overviews and background analyses of the major issues in the election, as well as the basic positions advocated by the candidates. This kind of reporting will provide the citizenry with the contextual information necessary to grasp the arguments advanced in the debates and will offer them a broader base of knowledge to assess what they have heard in the debates.

Many political observers, including many journalists, have observed that polling analyses, focus groups, and other survey techniques are certainly not sufficient to stimulate public discourse. We firmly agree with this view. Debates are moments in a campaign when the electorate has an opportunity to connect directly with the candidates. These events should therefore be presented in as unfiltered a manner as possible. *We therefore recommend that broadcasters and journalists enhance their debate night coverage to balance out the inevitable horse race figures and polling analyses that are included in such coverage.* Simply telling voters immediately after a debate the percentage of the electorate that approved or disapproved of a particular response, or the percentage that thought a particular candidate won, does not improve voter decisionmaking. Indeed, if anything, it discourages critical thinking and independent judgment on the part of the viewers. The public would be better served by coverage that incorporates more information about the issues raised in a debate and the viability of the candidates' respective proposals.

PROMOTE PUBLIC DISCUSSION OF THE DEBATES

News organizations and broadcast outlets can also enhance the value of the debates by undertaking activities that help to promote broader public discussion of these events. One way this end can be achieved is to report on public forums that bring together groups of citizens to watch and discuss the debates. The planning of such forums is already under way under the auspices of the Commission on Presidential Debates. The National Association of Broadcasters and many local media organizations have endorsed this effort and plan to assist in its implementation. We believe that these activities should be observed and watched closely. By covering these events and reporting citizens' views, media organizations can play an important role in stimulating public discussion of the debates and in generating a broader public dialogue about the election. They will also help to ensure that citizens have an expanded opportunity to share their views with others and take an active part in the political process.

We believe that such an effort can make a valuable contribution to the health of our political system. We live in a period when many citizens feel alienated from the electoral process and believe that their voices are not heard. By providing the citizenry with a formal means of coming together to discuss their views, we will give individuals a new way to participate in the process. Moreover, the Task Force feels that such sessions will help individuals learn from each other and form their own views regarding the debates, instead of having to base their opinions solely on polling data or the shotgun commentary of political observers that currently dominates postdebate news stories. *We therefore strongly support the establishment of programs designed to promote public viewing and discussion of the debates.* Such programs will enrich the public dialogue surrounding the debates and enhance the vitality of our democracy. By doing so, they will further legitimize the debates process and reinforce the importance of these forums in the presidential selection process. They will thus help to ensure that debates become a central institution of our political system for many years to come.

DISSENT AND SUPPLEMENTAL COMMENT

DISSENT

BY LAWRENCE K. GROSSMAN AND ELLEN HUME

We are strongly in favor of requiring presidential candidates to agree to participate in debates as a condition of accepting public campaign funding. Candidates who receive matching taxpayer campaign funds should be willing to debate their opponents on television, the vehicle that, as the Task Force says, affords voters the most valuable source of information to help them "cast a meaningful vote on election day."

The very purpose of public funding is to improve the candidates' ability to disseminate "their views on the problems facing the nation and set forth the policies they hope to pursue if elected to serve in office." Debates, we all agree, are the best means to accomplish that important goal. So why not use public funds to ensure that presidential debates actually take place?

Also of great importance, requiring an up-front commitment to debate from the major presidential candidates will help level the playing field for the vital negotiations that lead up to the debates. As we saw in 1992, as well as in all prior presidential campaigns, incumbents and front-runners invariably exercise undue influence and control over the debate terms and conditions. They hold an unfair advantage in influencing the debate schedule, formats, and arrangements. In some cases that influence has derailed presidential campaign debates altogether. In other cases, most recently in 1992, the incumbent's negotiating advantage came shockingly close to aborting the debates, and did end up undercutting the preparation time.

Requiring an up-front commitment for presidential debates in return for public campaign funding would set a strong example for the encouragement of televised debates at state and local campaign levels as well.

Our colleagues on the Task Force agree that debates are the most effective and important elements in presidential election campaigns, but they fail to recommend the one step that will do the most to ensure that presidential debates actually take place. They would leave candidates free to use taxpayer money to serve their own campaign ends, by spending the millions they receive from the federal Treasury on negative-attack TV spots, for example. Yet they avoid requiring those presidential candidates who benefit from the public's campaign largesse to make a good-faith commitment to serve the voters' best interest by appearing with their competitors and directly presenting their views to a nationwide audience.

Some argue that requiring candidates who accept public matching funds to commit to debate would infringe on their First Amendment rights. We don't believe that. Anyone who wants to keep silent can turn down federal campaign funding. After all, how does a presidential candidate's decision to refuse to debate serve free speech? The purpose of providing public funds is not to limit, censor, or regulate campaign debates, but to encourage them to happen, no matter how far ahead in the polls a presidential candidate may happen to be. The requirement to debate is consistent with the very purpose of public campaign financing, to promote substantive political dialogue among citizens, not to inhibit or reduce that dialogue. Presidential candidates who decide not to risk a public debate, or who insist on debating only on their own terms, do not deserve to be rewarded with taxpayers' campaign funds.

Supplemental Comment

by David A. Norcross

The word "guarantee" appears frequently in the Report. It is inappropriate. There are no guarantees in politics, nor should there be; guarantees are for constitutions and commercial products. The use of the word in this context suggests certainties that, while beguiling, do not exist in elective politics.

Likewise, the "authority" of the Commission raises a misleading notion. It is not the Commission's authority to compel debates that makes the process work; rather, it is the public demand for debates that compels candidates to debate. Accordingly, the strengthening of the Commission's presence and its continued success will enable the Commission to exert its influence to advantage but will not confer upon it any "authority."

I disagree that production of four presidential and one vice presidential forums has mystical significance and am content to let the Commission and the candidates negotiate the number of meetings that seem appropriate for the year in question. There are an ever increasing number and variety of forums available, some of which we may well have not even considered at this time. It makes no sense to establish such a requirement.

I would have made the conclusion regarding the "town hall meeting" debate somewhat less effusive. It was a very interesting setting but it also has significant problems, not the least of which is the selection of the audience-inquirers. I would not agree that it should be a central feature of future debates.

I strongly disagree with any requirement preventing candidates from participation in the selection of participating journalists. At the least, candidates should be permitted a limited number of "peremptory challenges." Personalities do play a significant role in politics and to pretend otherwise is foolish.

BACKGROUND PAPER
BY ANTHONY CORRADO

INTRODUCTION

The 1992 election represented the latest episode in an emerging democratic tradition. For the fifth consecutive presidential race, nationally televised debates were held between the major contenders for the country's highest office. But the 1992 debates were unique in many ways. For the first time they featured a forum in which the presidential candidates faced voters directly to answer their questions about the major issues confronting the nation. The 1992 debates also provided the electorate with its first opportunity to see a major independent candidate, Ross Perot, share the stage with an incumbent president, George Bush, and the Democratic nominee, Bill Clinton, on live national television. These innovations prompted extraordinary public interest in the debates, making them one of the most widely viewed political events in modern broadcast history. Those who did watch found them to be highly informative, and on election day more than half of those who cast their votes said the debates played a crucial role in helping them determine how to cast their ballot.

The 1992 experience thus reaffirmed what many scholars and political observers have been arguing for years: that nationally televised debates are an essential vehicle for informing voters about the candidates for president and vice president, and about their views on the issues. Numerous studies conducted over the past three decades have shown that debates make a substantial contribution to the quality of American democracy. These analyses have demonstrated that debates provide the public with greater information about the issue positions of the candidates than they receive from news accounts and candidate advertising; that they motivate some voters to revise their opinions on the major issues of the day and reassess their feelings toward the presidential and vice presidential hopefuls; that for others they tend to reinforce existing party and candidate loyalties; and lead still others to change their minds as to which candidate to support. Debates therefore help produce a more firmly committed, better-informed electorate, an essential component of a healthy and vital democracy.

That voters consider debates to be an important aid to their decisionmaking is reflected in the findings of public opinion polls on the topic. Every major survey of public attitudes toward debates conducted over the past two decades has found that a vast majority of the electorate not only wants but expects the major contenders for the nation's highest office to present their views in nationally televised forums. This attitude is grounded in the basic democratic belief that candidates should be accountable to the electorate and are obliged to share their views so that voters know where they stand on the issues that concern them most. The public does deserve to hear the candidates' views on these issues and candidates are obliged to address their concerns. But unfortunately, in recent campaigns the public's agenda has often been overshadowed by campaign strategies that emphasized negative campaign ads and attacks on the opposition. In fact, the public's concerns might not have received much attention at all were it not for the debates, which gave representatives of the public a formal opportunity to confront the candidates with their questions.

This desire to see the candidates oppose each other in face-to-face meetings is also a manifestation of the public's growing experience with debates. Indeed, one of the fundamental changes in our political system, too often overlooked, is that over the past two decades televised candidate debates have become a common feature of the electoral process. Less than thirty years ago, candidate debates were a rarity and were virtually unheard of in presidential races. Today they are a staple of presidential contests, with dozens of debates or other types of multicandidate forums held during the primary campaign in addition to those conducted during the general election. The success of these forums has encouraged candidates, journalists, and others to call for similar showcases in election contests for other federal, state, and local offices. As a result, debates are now the norm, not the exception, in congressional, gubernatorial, and mayoral politics, as well as in presidential races. Debates have proved to be so popular in campaigns that they are now even beginning to enter other aspects of American politics, as indicated by the debates on selected topics occasionally staged by members of Congress and broadcast by C-SPAN, or the "debate" (it was actually more of a joint guest appearance) between Vice President Al Gore and Ross Perot on the North American Free Trade Agreement that was hosted by Larry King on his nationally televised evening talk show.

Debates have also become an integral part of the electoral process because they are regarded by the public, the candidates, and the media alike as defining moments in a campaign. History has demonstrated that debates can have a significant influence on the dynamics of an election and shape the course of a campaign. Because most voters lack the time to follow the presidential race closely and do not want to rely on political ads for their information, they look to the debates as a primary means of learning about the candidates. A significant portion of the public therefore waits until after debates have been held to make a final decision about the candidates. They want to see and hear the candidates themselves, and then make a decision that incorporates any new information they might obtain. This tendency explains why presidential candidates place so much emphasis on the debates in developing their campaign strategies.

Candidates recognize the importance voters place on these forums and understand that no event during the course of a presidential campaign receives as much attention or is so widely watched as a general election debate. The debates thus provide the major party nominees with a unique opportunity to make their positions known and defend their views before millions of prospective voters. This can be especially important for a challenger facing an incumbent president, since the debates are the only venue in which the challenger will have a chance to share the stage and engage the president directly before a national audience.

Regardless of their status, candidates want to make the most of the opportunities afforded by debates, and they spend long hours preparing for these confrontations. They view the debates as critical contests in which they will be asked to discuss the issues in a pressure-filled situation that will be perceived as a test of their capacity to serve as president. Candidates who seize these opportunities and use them effectively to convey their views are likely to gain support and momentum, and may even win the presidency. Debates thus serve as inducements for candidates to work with their staffs to hone their campaign messages, prepare to discuss a wide range of issues, and think through their opponents' positions, all of which can help to improve a candidate's effectiveness in communicating with voters.

Both the candidates and the public have come to regard them as so important that debates now exert a significant influence on the dynamics of a presidential campaign. For example, the standard fare of daily campaign activity essentially comes to a halt in the days leading up to a debate because the candidates are focusing on debate preparation and a sizable share of the electorate wants to wait to see the debate before making any further decisions. Some observers, mostly campaign strategists and a few journalists, have even suggested that one of the problems with debates is that they tend to "freeze" the campaign and that this effect should be considered in planning such forums. This charge, however, contains little merit. Even if debates do bring "normal" campaigning to a halt for a few days, the value of these events with respect to the public interest and the informational needs of the electorate far outweighs the potential benefit of almost any other activity a candidate might undertake on the campaign trail, especially if the trade-off simply entails the loss of a few more appearances in a few more media markets or a few more days of political advertising. Debates should be one of the dominant activities in a presidential campaign, and that they are seen as such should not be an argument against them. Indeed, the quality of future campaigns would be significantly improved if the candidates and the public spent more time preparing for debates and devoted even greater attention to these forums than they have in the past.

Because presidential debates are such crucial events in so important a contest, they have been subjected to intensive public scrutiny. Ever since the first nationally televised general election debates, the "Great Debates" between John F. Kennedy and Richard M. Nixon in 1960, scholarly analysts, political experts, and other commentators have been engaged in continuous efforts to determine their consequences, as well as to identify ways to improve their value as an educational tool for voters. These analyses have generated substantial controversy. For the most part, the criticisms advanced against debates center on the effects of these forums and the procedures under which they are conducted.

Some scholars, for example, argue that the debates have not achieved their full potential as a vehicle for promoting a well-informed electorate because the information they convey is largely associated with the style and manner of the candidates, the "image" presented on the television screen, and is too often reduced to brief quips, snappy one-liners, and other short takes that do little to advance the viewer's understanding of complicated public policy issues. Most of the critics attribute this problem to the way the press reports on the debates. The press, like other participants in the process, devotes substantial attention to the debates, both before and after they take place. Reporters analyze their every dimension in hopes of attaining some insight into the dynamics of the race and the keys that will determine the election's outcome. The coverage, however, usually concentrates on the candidates' respective strategies, their specific tactics, and on who won or lost. Reporters tend to cast the debates as part of a larger game to win the Oval Office, instead of treating them as part of a dialogue about policy issues that can help voters better understand the central issues in a particular election campaign. And in doing so, they rarely rely on any sort of an objective standard. Instead they determine winners and losers by relying on the views of analysts, campaign staffers, polls, and even their fellow journalists. As a result, the coverage generally serves to undermine the educational value of the debates rather than enhance it.

These concerns have led some academic observers to question the effects of debates on overall voting patterns, since some studies suggest that voters' reactions are based more on the images generated by the debates and news coverage surrounding them than on the substance of the statements made during the actual events. Still others have argued that the debates have had little apparent effect on election outcomes, particularly since many academic studies have found it hard to separate the effects of the debates from other forces and events that influence voter opinion.

The process by which debates are arranged and their logistics have also been criticized. Some observers charge that control of the process has shifted from debate sponsors to the candidates themselves, who essentially determine the major procedural and logistical details and try to manipulate the setup to further their own political interests. As a result, say these analysts, with each ensuing election, these forums have proved to be less of an educational vehicle for voters and more of a political tool used by the candidates to serve their own purposes. In support of this contention, many observers have cited the predominant use of a modified press conference format in which candidates answer questions posed by journalists, which they say stifles the type of argumentation and clash between candidates that would be most meaningful to voters. The 1992 debates represented a major advance in this regard since they moved away from the press panel by employing a single moderator in some of the debates and a highly innovative town hall meeting approach in another. But some feel that even with these changes there are still too many governing restrictions and guidelines. Many of these individuals, for example, would prefer forums that encourage actual debate between the candidates; that is, formats that promote more freewheeling discourse, in which candidates respond directly to each other, ask questions of each other, and offer replies to each other's statements with a single moderator to introduce topics and guide the conversation. Such an approach, advocates claim, would produce more confrontation between candidates, force them to forsake standard stump speeches, and give voters a better sense of the differences between them.

Ironically, many of these procedural criticisms are related to the success of the debates. Because these forums are such important moments in national elections, they are a focal point of attention for the major participants in the electoral process. The prestige of the debates make them an event that many organizations would like to sponsor, leading to disputes among competing organizations, as well as controversies over the type of organization or particular group best suited to stage these forums. Their demonstrable impact on voter perceptions has encouraged the candidates to try to exert as much control as possible over the arrangements that give shape to the debates, which has led to complicated conflicts between the candidates and prospective sponsors, between the sponsors and the networks that cover the debates, and, perhaps most importantly, among the candidates themselves. Such disputes have highlighted the political and partisan dimensions of the debates, and have therefore led some voters and many neutral organizations to question whether such spectacles best serve the public interest.

Despite these criticisms, it is important to note that there is nearly unanimous agreement among observers and participants that the debates are a valuable addition to the electoral process and should become a permanent fixture in presidential campaigns. Even the most severe critics acknowledge the value of debates as a means of improving American elections. There is also wide agreement that the 1992 debates were the best held to date, representing a major improvement over those staged previously. They provided the voters with what they were looking for: a chance to see the major candidates discuss the issues in different settings and under varied formats. The second debate, which took the form of a "town hall meeting," was especially important in that it gave a select group of citizens an unparalleled opportunity to participate directly in the presidential selection process. This exercise in direct democracy, broadcast to a national audience, indicates the role debates can serve in promoting a sense of efficacy and connectedness to the political system among voters who have in recent years become increasingly alienated and distrustful of the political process.

But, even with the success of the 1992 forums, there are further improvements that should be considered to ensure that debates continue to be as meaningful as possible in future elections. This goal is best met by continuing to study the history of presidential debates and examining the strengths and weaknesses of various proposals for reforming them. Such analysis can deepen public understanding, highlight the benefits and disadvantages of different alternatives, encourage innovative thinking, and maintain an ongoing public dialogue about ways to enhance the quality of the electoral process and the vitality of our democracy. It is with these objectives in mind that this background paper was written.

CHAPTER ONE

PRESIDENTIAL DEBATES:
A BRIEF HISTORY

Public debates between candidates seeking the presidency of the United States are a distinctly modern phenomenon. Although American democracy has a long tradition of open political debate, throughout the nineteenth century few candidates for elective office met their opponents face to face to discuss the issues. This was especially true of presidential aspirants, who generally adhered to the pre-Jacksonian notion that personal campaigning was beneath the dignity of the nation's highest office. Debating was an activity primarily associated with legislative deliberations, a practice undertaken by great statesmen in addressing the major issues of the day. The most memorable debates of the nineteenth century were those that took place in the Congress, such as the debate between Senators Daniel Webster and Robert Hayne in 1830 over the nature of the union of states or the debate among Webster, Henry Clay, and John C. Calhoun over the Compromise of 1850 and the extension of slavery into newly admitted states and territories.

The major exception to this rule was the series of debates between Abraham Lincoln and Stephen Douglas in the 1858 Senate election in Illinois. In this now famous instance, Lincoln and Douglas agreed to participate in seven debates in seven different congressional districts, usually with one of them addressing an audience in the afternoon and the other later that day. Each debate was scheduled for three hours, with the first candidate speaking for an hour and the second for an hour and a half, followed by the first returning for the final half hour. The initial debate took place in Ottawa on August 21, 1858, and the others followed at intervals ranging from two days to more than two weeks. Most of their arguments were devoted to the question of slavery, the major issue confronting the nation, and they provided their audiences with an almost exhaustive discussion of the legal arguments involved in the question of extending slavery into the territories, as well as the Supreme Court's ruling in the Dred Scott case. The debates highlighted the areas of agreement and disagreement between the candidates, and were closely followed by the public and widely reported in newspapers.

The Lincoln-Douglas debates were so widely attended that they have become a part of our political mythology. But they did not change the ways candidates for major office sought election. Few candidates followed their example, and they produced no public demand for more debates. It was not until the emergence of radio and television broadcasting as a primary means of communicating with the electorate that presidential contenders, realizing the potential value of these technologies as vehicles for airing their views and providing a forum for direct confrontations with their opponents, began to think seriously about incorporating debates into the campaign.[1]

Experiments with presidential campaign broadcast debates began as early as 1948, when Thomas E. Dewey and Harold Stassen, candidates for the Republican presidential nomination, held a one-hour radio debate on a single issue, the outlawing of communism in the United States, four days before the crucial Oregon primary. This encounter, which was conducted in a radio studio, featured twenty-minute opening statements and eight-and-a-half-minute rebuttals from each candidate. Broadcast nationwide by the ABC, NBC, and Mutual Broadcasting System radio networks, the forum attracted an estimated audience of between 40 and 80 million listeners.[2] This debate "played a role in the undoing of Stassen's presidential bid,"[3] as Dewey subsequently won the primary by a narrow margin, and "his victory generally was believed to have eliminated Stassen from the presidential race."[4] But despite the apparent public interest, there was no serious consideration of a general election debate between Dewey and President Harry Truman.

In the next two presidential elections, candidates began to experiment with televised debates during the primary campaign but only on a limited basis. In what might be considered a precursor to modern debates, a number of Democratic and Republican contenders (or their representatives) appeared together in May 1952 in a nationally televised event staged at the annual convention of the League of Women Voters. The participants were asked two questions, one on ways to prevent government dishonesty and inefficiency, and another on whether to increase or decrease foreign economic assistance.[5] Two months later, Senator Blair Moody of Michigan made the first specific suggestion for televised debates between the presidential nominees, proposing that one of the television networks or some other organization host a series of debates between Adlai Stevenson and Dwight Eisenhower. Both NBC and CBS offered time for debates and sent invitations to the candidates, but neither candidate accepted the network offers.[6]

In 1956, Stevenson did participate in a debate with Estes Kefauver, his principal opponent for the Democratic Party presidential nomination. This hour-long forum was the first nationally telecast intraparty debate, and was broadcast by ABC on May 21, eight days before the Florida primary. Stevenson felt compelled to make the appearance because Kefauver had won the Minnesota primary, and analysts at the time believed that the Florida results were likely to determine the outcomes of the rest of the spring primaries. The debate, however, was generally regarded as dull and indecisive. Stevenson won the state, but his debate experience seemed to dampen his enthusiasm for a similar opportunity in the general election. Even if he had wanted to, it is unlikely that such a debate would have been held, since the extremely popular Eisenhower was disinclined to participate in a televised encounter with his opponent.[7] Accordingly, as in 1952, no joint appearance of Eisenhower and Stevenson took place during the 1956 general election.

Besides the wariness of candidates as to the value of debates, the early experience with these types of forums was also hampered by the uncertainties generated by Section 315 of the Federal Communications Act, the so-called equal time rule.[8] Under this provision, a federally licensed broadcast station that makes time available to the Republican and Democratic candidates for elective office must make an equal amount of time available to all other legally qualified candidates, regardless of the size of their parties or their levels of public support. This requirement made broadcasters hesitant to offer time to the major-party nominees in the general election because, under the original interpretation of the law, any appearance by a candidate for public office on television could trigger the equal time provision. The broadcasters were justified in their concern, especially given their experience with the law in the 1950s. In 1959, for example, the Federal Communications Commission ruled that a minor candidate for mayor of Chicago, Lar Daly, had to be given an equal opportunity to respond to twenty-one seconds of news coverage of incumbent mayor Richard Daley's airport greeting of the president of Argentina.[9] Broadcasters thus feared that any appearance by a presidential candidate would force them to give time to other aspirants, which would reduce their advertising revenues by filling up time slots that could otherwise be sold or by forcing them to alter their regularly scheduled programming.

In response to this concern, Congress amended Section 315 in 1959, exempting broadcasters from the equal time rule for coverage of political candidates, so long as the televised appearance was either a "bona fide newscast," "a bona fide news interview," "a bona fide news documentary," or "on the spot coverage of a bona fide news event." Whether debates met any one of these conditions, however, was still at issue even after this change was adopted. So on August 22, 1960, Congress passed a resolution initiated in the Senate to suspend Section 315 during the 1960 general election period.[10] With this legislative hurdle cleared, the stage was set for the first nationally televised, presidential general election debates, the "Great Debates" of 1960.

THE 1960 DEBATES

On the eve of the Republican National Convention's nomination of Richard Nixon, which followed the nomination of John Kennedy by the Democrats, NBC issued an invitation to both candidates to participate in a series of eight one-hour debates during the course of the general election, which the network called the "Great Debates." This proposal included six joint appearances by Nixon and Kennedy, a joint appearance by their vice presidential running mates, and a program featuring the minor-party candidates. Soon thereafter, ABC and CBS also extended invitations to the candidates to appear on evening prime-time television for a series of debates.

Kennedy was the first to accept NBC's invitation, followed closely by Nixon. Nixon suggested that since the other networks had put forth similar offers, the three networks should coordinate their proposals.[11] The candidates readily agreed to debate because each thought these appearances would be personally beneficial. Nixon, a skilled debater, felt that he could use television successfully, as he had demonstrated in his 1952 "Checkers" speech. Kennedy was also comfortable with television and believed that he could use the planned broadcasts to address the major obstacle confronting his campaign, the impression that he was young and lacked the experience needed to carry out the responsibilities of the nation's highest office.[12]

The details of the debates were worked out in protracted negotiations between the candidates' advisers and representatives of CBS, NBC, ABC, and the Mutual Broadcasting System. Initially, an attempt was made to use the format of the 1948 Dewey-Stassen debate, but both campaigns rejected this proposal because they felt that there was no single dominant issue in the election and that such a debate would draw little interest. The networks also suggested a forum in which the candidates could question each other, but both candidates vetoed this proposal as well. Disputes also arose over the types of camera shots that could be used (for example, candidate reaction shots, which Kennedy favored, were allowed, but left-side profiles of Nixon and shots of a candidate wiping his brow were not).[13]

After twelve meetings, the negotiators reached a final agreement in mid-September, which called for four one-hour, nationally televised joint appearances by the candidates to be held on September 26, and October 7, 13, and 21. These appearances were to be broadcast simultaneously on all three television networks and four radio networks with the specific sponsor of each debate determined by lot.[14] All were held in television studios, with a panel of journalists asking questions of the candidates and a moderator to conduct the proceedings. Each debate provided for rebuttals by the candidates but did not allow the panelists to ask follow-up questions. In addition to panel questioning, the first and fourth debates included opening and closing statements by the candidates and were limited to specific topics, with the first meeting dedicated to domestic issues and the fourth to foreign affairs. The second and third debates were open to any subject. In three of the four debates, the candidates would appear side by side, at varying distances, in a television studio. For the third debate, Kennedy was in New York and Nixon in Los Angeles due to their campaign scheduling, so they participated from their respective locations and their images were joined on the television screen.

The debates generated unprecedented public attention. Approximately 90 percent of the potential viewing audience, or more than 100 million Americans, saw at least one of the encounters, and the average audience for the four debates was about 71 million viewers.

Approximately 53.1 percent of the potential audience watched three of the four.[15] Another 10 million listened to the discussion on radio.[16] This extraordinary level of public interest was not simply the result of a captive audience, since the debate viewership was 20 percent greater than the usual audience for the programs they replaced.[17] It was also in part due to the unique character of these appearances; never before had the American public had an opportunity to watch the major presidential nominees discuss election issues in a shared forum from the comfort of their own homes.

Nixon

What most impressed these viewers, and what is most remembered about the 1960 debates, were the "images" presented by the first debate, which was held in Chicago. Nixon, who had a painful knee injury and had just recovered from an unfortunately timed case of the flu that caused him to lose weight, appeared tired and pale on the screen. He refused professional makeup and therefore looked pasty and poorly shaven, with deep shadows under his eyes. His gray suit offered little contrast against the gray background of the studio set, and his eyes darted nervously between Kennedy, the moderator, and camera. As campaign journalist Theodore White later noted, "everything that could have gone wrong that night [for Nixon] went wrong."[18] The telegenic Kennedy, on the other hand, looked rested, tanned, and vigorous. He wore a dark suit and had been coached in how to sit (legs crossed) and where to look when not speaking (at Nixon).[19] Kennedy also proved to be the more aggressive candidate, putting Nixon on the defensive and directly taking on the issue of his relative inexperience by discussing his career in Congress.

Kennedy

Most observers considered Kennedy to have won the debate, but this assessment was rarely based on the substance of the debate, that is, on responses to the panelists' questions. In fact, the *New York Times* reported that "on sound points of argument, Nixon probably took most of the honors."[20] Television, however, is a visual medium, and it was Nixon's image, juxtaposed with Kennedy's, that had the greater influence on viewer opinion.[21] The contrast was so stark that the television audience generally gained a different impression of the candidates than did the radio audience. According to one study, those who heard the debate only on radio judged it to be a draw, while those who watched on television gave Kennedy a solid victory.[22]

Nixon was more effective in the later debates. By the second debate, he demonstrated that he had learned the lessons of Chicago by wearing a dark suit and proper makeup. The most dramatic moment in this debate was the confrontation between the candidates on the defense of two small, Taiwan-controlled islands off of the Chinese mainland, Quemoy and Matsu. Nixon took advantage of this discussion to highlight his foreign policy expertise and accused Kennedy of "woolly thinking" on the issue. This issue, as well as other aspects of the conduct of the cold war, was also a focal point of subsequent debates, thus allowing Nixon to shore up his strength in the area of foreign policy and claim that Kennedy was weak in his willingness to contain communism.

But Nixon's later performances were not enough to overcome the impression formed by the first debate, particularly given Kennedy's success in standing up to the vice president throughout the entire series. After the election, most observers, including the candidates themselves, felt that the debates had played a crucial role in providing Kennedy with his narrow margin of victory. A Roper poll conducted at the time substantiated this view. It revealed that 57 percent of those who voted said that the debates had influenced their decision. Of these respondents, 6 percent said that their final decision was based on the debates alone, with 72 percent of this group voting for Kennedy and 26 percent for Nixon.[23] A study by Kurt and Gladys Engel Lang further found that the debates had the effect of reinforcing voters' previous inclinations and preferences, and thus helped to firm up their opinions concerning which candidate to support.[24]

After the election, most observers heralded this new addition to the presidential selection process as the beginning of a political tradition of great value to voters. The debates had clearly proved to be of substantial interest to the electorate and were expected to change the future of presidential campaigns. Walter Lippman, for instance, declared that "the TV debate was a bold innovation which is bound to be carried forward into future campaigns, and could not now be abandoned. From now on, it will be impossible for any candidate for any important office to avoid this kind of confrontation."[25] Two years later, Nixon admitted the same, saying that "debates between the presidential candidates are a fixture, and in all the elections in the future we are going to have debates between the candidates."[26]

This certainty, however, proved to be short-lived; no debates were held in the next three presidential election campaigns. As planning began for the 1964 campaign, Kennedy appeared ready to participate in debates, and legislation was circulating in Congress to suspend Section 315 once again. But after Kennedy's death, President Lyndon

Johnson showed no interest in sharing the stage with his opponent, Barry Goldwater, especially since Johnson had a commanding lead early in the race and did not want to provide his challenger with a national platform that might elevate his status. He therefore made sure that Congress, which was controlled by the Democrats, did not adopt legislation to revoke or suspend the equal time rule. In 1968, Richard Nixon, still mindful of his 1960 experience, had no intention of debating Democrat Hubert Humphrey and was particularly anxious to avoid giving additional exposure to independent candidate George Wallace, whom Humphrey had suggested should be included in any debate.[27] Nixon successfully dodged a number of proposals for joint appearances, and Senate Republicans blocked a bill to suspend Section 315, thus making the issue easier to avoid. In 1972, Nixon maintained his stance en route to his landslide reelection victory and refused to debate George McGovern.

THE 1976 DEBATES

After a sixteen-year hiatus, a number of circumstances combined in 1976 to make a return of the debates possible. First, in 1975, the Federal Communications Commission reinterpreted the equal time rule in response to a petition by the Aspen Institute, a public affairs foundation.[28] The Commission's Aspen Institute decision radically changed the attitude of broadcasters toward debates since it allowed encounters between political candidates without regard to the equal time provision so long as the program qualified as a "bona fide news event," was initiated by a nonbroadcast entity, and was covered live and in its entirety.[29] This eliminated the need for legislation to suspend Section 315 and paved the way for future debates. In 1983, the Commission expanded this ruling by deciding to allow networks and local broadcasters the privilege of sponsorship, which it hoped would serve to increase the number of broadcast debates.[30]

Second, the League of Women Voters emerged as a sponsor. During the 1976 primaries, the League, through its affiliated Education Fund, conducted four nationally televised debates, each with a specific theme, among the contenders for the Democratic nomination. In May, the organization decided to launch a campaign for general election debates. It led a petition drive and established an administering body to conduct the debates. Following these actions, it began to meet with advisers to the prospective party nominees, and in August it publicly invited the candidates to participate in a series of debates during the general election.[31]

Finally, in marked contrast to previous elections, both candidates felt that it was in their interest to debate. Gerald Ford, who had been elevated from the Congress to the vice presidency after Spiro Agnew's resignation and then succeeded to the presidency when Nixon resigned, was the only unelected president in American history. Although his public standing was high soon after he became president, his support declined as a result of his unpopular decision to pardon Nixon and an increasingly poor public image. By the time of the Republican National Convention, he trailed Democrat Jimmy Carter by a large margin, and his advisers decided that he should take the bold step of challenging his opponent to a series of debates, which he did in his acceptance speech at the convention. At about the same time, Carter was preparing his own debate proposal. While ahead in the polls, Carter was still relatively unknown to the majority of the electorate, and his advisers discerned some apprehension among voters as to whether he was qualified to be president.[32] Accordingly, Carter took up Ford's challenge the day after it was issued, as well as the League's invitation, to which Ford had already responded favorably before delivering his acceptance speech. The Democrats also decided to meet a challenge offered by Ford's running mate, Robert Dole, to hold a debate between the number-two men on the ticket. Thus, for the first time, an incumbent president would participate in debates and the public would be treated to a forum between the vice presidential candidates.

The details were worked out in two meetings between the candidates' representatives and the League's Steering Committee. While fewer meetings were needed than in 1960 to arrange the debates, the sessions were much more combative. The candidates sparred over a range of issues, including whether Ford's lectern would be adorned with the presidential seal and whether the networks would be allowed to broadcast audience reaction shots. The candidates decided against both of these practices. They also refused the League's suggestion to allow time for the candidates to ask questions of each other, preferring instead to retain the "less risky" panel format used in 1960.[33] Controversy also arose over the candidates' demand that they have a role in selecting the panel participants; the League opposed such interference but allowed each candidate to submit a list of suggested questioners for its consideration.[34]

These negotiations resulted in a series of four debates: three ninety-minute forums between the presidential candidates held on September 23, October 6, and October 22, and one seventy-five-minute vice presidential face-off held on October 15. The first presidential debate was devoted to domestic policy, the second to foreign policy, and the third open to any topic. The debates broke away from the 1960 precedent by allowing follow-up questions from the moderators, candidate rebuttals, and closing statements in each of the sessions. Also, instead of being held in television studios, the debates were to be broadcast from public locations, such as theaters or auditoriums, and conducted before an audience.[35]

The debates again attracted substantial public interest. According to Nielsen Media Research statistics, the first one was watched by an impressive 51.6 million households, or about 146 million persons.[36] An estimated 160 million Americans, and 250 million people across the world, saw at least part of the debates.[37] What many of these observers probably remembered most, however, was not the arguments offered by the candidates or their positions on particular issues, but two odd moments, one of which had an enduring impact on candidate attitudes toward debates.

The first significant incident took place during the initial debate in Philadelphia, where the candidates discussed domestic policy and economic issues. According to most reports, Ford performed well in this encounter, as he cast Carter as a big spender and attacked him for lacking specifics in his policy proposals while highlighting his own experience and his differences with Carter on tax policy, energy conservation, and the pardoning of Vietnam War draft resisters. But what stood out most was the response of the candidates to a long delay that occurred near the end of the debate. As a result of an equipment malfunction, the sound on stage went dead for twenty-seven minutes. During this period, neither candidate moved, presumably because they were afraid that they might be caught on camera in an unflattering pose, an awkward stare, or some other action that might be judged "nonpresidential."[38] The breakdown also forced the networks to decide whether to end their transmission or stay, a decision that was influenced by the 1975 Aspen ruling, which dictated that broadcasters' only role was to cover debates, not create them.[39] So for almost a half hour, the nation watched the two candidates as they stood at their podiums, eyes fixed straight ahead, waiting for the technicians to fix the problem and the debate to resume. Some observers speculated that the candidates had learned, perhaps too well, the lesson of the Kennedy-Nixon debate: that image can be as important as substance.[40]

The other significant incident occurred in the second debate in San Francisco, which was devoted to foreign policy. Although Ford was expected to do well in this debate and did in fact continue to berate Carter for speaking in broad generalities, Carter appeared more confident, engaging the president on such topics as human rights and American prestige abroad and accusing Ford of surrendering the leadership of foreign policy to Secretary of State Henry Kissinger. The substance of Carter's remarks, however, was overshadowed by an apparent misstatement Ford made in an exchange with Max Frankel of the *New York Times* concerning Soviet influence in Eastern Europe. In response to a question asked by Frankel, Ford declared: "There is no Soviet domination of Eastern Europe, and there never will be under a Ford administration." Frankel, who appeared surprised by the statement, rejoined: "I'm sorry . . . did I understand you to say, sir, that the Soviets are not using Eastern Europe as their own sphere of influence in occupying most of the countries there? . . ." To which Ford responded:

> I don't believe, Mr. Frankel, that the Yugoslavians consider themselves dominated by the Soviet Union. I don't believe that the Rumanians consider themselves dominated by the Soviet Union. I don't believe that the Poles consider themselves dominated by the Soviet Union. Each of these countries is independent, autonomous, it has its own territorial integrity, and the United States does not concede that those countries are under the domination of the Soviet Union.

The press immediately seized upon Ford's statement as a major blunder, with one report describing it as "the blooper heard 'round the world."[41] Ford, however, stood by his claim, and news reports of the debate were dominated by discussions of the exchange and its potential effect on the race. These postdebate discussions ultimately had a significant impact on voter opinion. In polls conducted immediately after the debate, only about 10 percent of respondents mentioned Ford's statement as a turning point in the debate; but in later interviews, after repeated media telecasts of the exchange, it was mentioned by almost 60 percent of respondents.[42] A study found that between noon and midnight on the day following the event, a period in which Ford's statement was widely broadcast and reported, the percentage of viewers declaring Ford the winner of the debate dropped from 31 to 19 percent, while the percentage naming Carter the winner rose from 44 to 61 percent.[43]

As in 1960, the debates proved to be a turning point in the presidential race. Most observers felt that the debates were the key to Carter's narrow electoral victory and that Ford's misstep might have cost him the race. The importance of the debates in determining the final outcome was summarized by R. W. Apple of the *New York Times*, who noted that it was "highly probable that had the President not stumbled over a question about Eastern Europe in the second debate, costing his campaign 10 days of momentum, the outcome would have been reversed."[44]

The 1976 experience demonstrated once again the public enthusiasm for debates and their potential importance in determining electoral outcomes. It also played a role in guaranteeing future debates. According to political communications specialist Robert Friedenberg, "the 1976 election was pivotal in the institutionalization of political debates for three reasons."[45] First, the election marked the first time an incumbent president (albeit unelected) participated in debating. Moreover, the public's response to the candidates demonstrated that debates do not necessarily disadvantage an incumbent; while Carter's status was elevated by sharing the stage with the president, Ford improved his standing in the polls throughout the debate period. Second, the election featured the first vice presidential debate, which was viewed by an estimated 100 million people.[46] Although this encounter had no demonstrable effect on the election outcome, it substantiated the view that the public was also interested in seeing the other candidates on the ticket spar verbally on the issues. Finally, since Carter had eagerly pursued debates in 1976, it would be difficult for him to avoid them if he sought reelection, thus creating for the first time the likelihood of debates in consecutive elections.

Some commentators, however, were less sanguine about the 1976 proceedings. While they acknowledged that the revival of debates had made a major contribution to the presidential race and had a measurable influence on voter opinion, they felt that the major legacy of the debates was to teach candidates to fear verbal gaffes and to encourage them to be more cautious in the future. As David Lanoue and Peter Schrott have written, the new lesson of the 1976 presidential debates was that the gaffe was deadly and must be avoided at all costs. Certainly, the media began increasingly to focus attention on such verbal miscues. From 1976 on, one feature of post-debate commentary would be to speculate on whether any gaffes had been committed. Further, the debates after 1976 were marked by more extensive coaching and well-packaged answers, motivated by a real fear of spontaneity.[47]

Critical commentary was also directed at the formats employed in the debates. Observers argued that the press panel approach gave participants too little time to respond to questions, stifled confrontation between the candidates, and confused the role of journalists by allowing them to participate in an event they were supposed to be covering.[48] The League's handling of the debates was another source of controversy, since some felt that the arrangements were largely determined by the candidates, not the sponsor. Media analysts Herbert Seltz and Richard Yoakam, for instance, claimed that "when the time came for the broadcasts, the League and the networks produced events tailored by and for the candidates. The League accomplished its goal of presenting debates, but at a price."[49]

THE 1980 DEBATES

Early in 1980 it appeared that the promise of 1976 would be readily fulfilled as both Ronald Reagan and President Carter declared their willingness to participate in general election debates. The idea, however, soon became ensnared in the question of whether independent candidate John Anderson would be invited to participate. Anderson, who had lost the race for the Republican Party nomination to Reagan, announced his intention to run as an independent in the general election well before the primaries were over. Throughout the summer he showed surprising strength in public opinion polls, with his support hovering around 20 percent.[50] The conventional wisdom at the time was that, nationwide, Anderson would take more votes away from Carter than he did from Reagan as long as his level of support was greater than 6 percent.[51]

Anderson's strong showing presented problems not only for the major-party candidates, but also for the League of Women Voters, which was planning once again to serve as sponsor. The League proposed a schedule of debates modeled on 1976, with three presidential forums and one vice presidential meeting. On August 10, the organization announced that it had established three criteria for determining whether a candidate would be invited to participate in these debates. These were: (1) constitutional eligibility to hold the office; (2) a place on the ballot in enough states to have a mathematical possibility of winning the election, namely, enough to furnish a majority of the votes in the electoral college; and (3) significant voter interest and support, which could be demonstrated by garnering the nomination of a major party or by receiving at least 15 percent voter support in nationwide public opinion polls.[52] The third criterion was particularly controversial, as many experts and pollsters argued that the standard was inadequate and represented an improper use of opinion polls.[53] But the League stuck by its decision, and on September 9 it announced that Anderson met the qualifications and would be invited to participate in the debates along with President Carter and Ronald Reagan.

Reagan and Anderson accepted the League's invitation, but Carter refused. Unwilling to participate in a debate against two candidates he considered Republicans, or to provide Anderson with a nationally televised forum that could elevate his status, Carter said that he would consider offers from other organizations to participate in a two-way debate with Reagan. But Reagan countered that he would agree to a debate only if Anderson were included. Despite constant public posturing by the candidates and attempts by the League to negotiate a compromise, this stalemate could not be broken. As a result, the League decided to hold the debate it had scheduled in Baltimore on September 21, with only Reagan and Anderson participating.

The Reagan-Anderson debate lasted sixty minutes and featured six main questions from a panel of journalists, with candidate rebuttals and closing statements. Carter's decision not to participate reduced the stature of the event, and only about 55 million Americans watched, which was less than half of the average audience for the 1976 debates.[54] But the debate did provide Anderson with the national attention he was seeking, and he took advantage of the opportunity to present some of his bold policy proposals, such as using higher gasoline taxes to promote conservation. Reagan also benefited from the debate. He used the forum to articulate his major campaign themes and to counteract the perception that he was too conservative for the majority of the electorate, a view the Carter campaign was trying to promote. Opinion polls conducted after the debate found that the forum "actually mitigated the characterization of Reagan as a conservative" since a smaller percentage of the public subsequently "characterized him as a strict ideologue on all issues."[55] More important, surveys indicated an increase in the percentage of voters who felt that Reagan understood the "complicated problems a President has to deal with," as well as an upswing in Reagan's public support, with Reagan converting a four-point deficit into a five-point lead over the president.[56] Anderson's appearance, however, failed to benefit his candidacy. Although he narrowly trailed Reagan in terms of the proportion of the electorate who thought he had won the debate, he did not receive the surge in public support he had hoped to gain from his appearance. Instead, his standing in the polls began to decline, and within two weeks he had fallen below 10 percent nationwide.[57]

With Anderson below 15 percent, the League announced in October that a two-way debate between Carter and Reagan was now possible. By this point some of Carter's advisers felt the president did not need to participate in a debate, but Carter accepted the League's invitation and agreed to appear in one ninety-minute debate on October 28, a week before the election. The debate immediately became the focal point of the campaign, and more than 120 million viewers decided to watch the confrontation.[58] In the debate, Carter stressed how his programs had benefited specific constituencies, cast Reagan as inexperienced and untested on military issues, and tried to heighten voter concern about a Reagan presidency by mentioning a discussion with his daughter Amy about the risks of nuclear proliferation. Reagan responded with detailed and moderate answers, noting several times his experience as governor of California, and fended off Carter's assaults by emphasizing the nation's poor economic condition and by implying that his positions were often being misrepresented by the president.

The postdebate news coverage tended to single out two of Reagan's brief statements as indicative of why he was considered the winner in the debate. The first was a response to the president's claim that Reagan would cut Medicare. Reagan began his answer with "There you go again," a remark meant to imply that Carter was misrepresenting his position. This statement, which was replayed a number of times in news broadcasts, was taken by some commentators as representative of Reagan's relaxed style and image, which contrasted sharply with Carter's more formal and intense appearance. The second was an excerpt from Reagan's closing statement, in which he asked: "Are you better off than you were four years ago?" This question was considered particularly effective by many observers since it summarized what many experts felt was the key issue in the race.[59] It also may have helped to crystallize voter discontent with the president, allowing Reagan to maintain his slim lead going into the final days of the election.

Carter felt that the debate played a crucial role in his losing the election. "I lost the debate," he said, "and that hurt badly."[60] Reagan took advantage of the opportunities afforded by the debates to address the concerns raised about his candidacy and to present his platform to the American people. His performance helped to convince millions of voters of his capacity to serve as president. One study, for example, found that only 6 percent of voters sampled had changed their vote on the basis of the Carter-Reagan debate, and those who did selected Reagan by a two-to-one margin.[61]

Some observers who shared the view that Carter had lost the confrontation argued that the debate had come so late in the campaign that Carter had little chance to make up ground after the event. As Lanoue and Schrott have observed,

> many observers considered the timing of the debate to be critical. Had the debate not taken place so close to election day, many felt, Carter might have had time to recover from its effects. The risks of debating were only magnified by the proximity of the event to the election; any mistakes would still be fresh on the minds of the voters as they cast their ballots. After 1980, candidates (particularly those ahead in the polls) would take care to schedule debates well in advance of election day.[62]

The 1980 experience also reinforced many of the criticisms that had emerged after the 1976 election. Analysts continued to argue that the debates emphasized style over substance, encouraged candidates to address complicated issues with snappy one-liners and other sound bites, and produced little confrontation between the contenders thanks to the use of the press panel format. Some also complained that the candidates continued to exercise too much control over the process, and that the press devoted too much time to the candidates' debate about whether to debate,[63] which resulted in less attention being given to the more important issues in the campaign. These same criticisms would become even more pronounced after each of the debates conducted over the next two election cycles.

THE 1984 DEBATES

On November 8, 1983, the Federal Communications Commission, despite objections from the League of Women Voters, finally loosened its restrictions on debate sponsorship by broadening its Aspen ruling to allow broadcast networks to serve as debate sponsors without triggering the equal time provision.[64] The decision prompted a number of national networks and local broadcasters to sponsor 1984 primary debates among the Democratic challengers, but the networks made no attempt to sponsor general election debates. This task was once again left to the League of Women Voters.

The League faced few of the difficulties it encountered in 1980 in getting the candidates' consent to appear. Although Reagan held a substantial lead in the polls in his quest for reelection, he "felt constrained to debate his challenger,"[65] former vice president Walter Mondale, even though he apparently had little to gain by doing so. The candidates also agreed that a vice presidential debate should be held. Debate expert Sidney Kraus has argued that this election "set a precedent for the institutionalization of presidential debates" because it was the first time an incumbent president with a large lead felt a responsibility to meet his opponent face to face and discuss the issues in a nationally televised forum.

A final agreement, however, was not achieved until September 17, after a series of intense negotiations. Most of the discussion centered on the details of the debates. Mondale's advisers began the bargaining with a request for six debates; Reagan's camp wanted only one.[66] Eventually, the campaigns agreed to three: two presidential showdowns, to be held on October 7 and 21, and one vice presidential forum on October 11. They also detailed many of the specific arrangements for the debates, including such items as set design, program format, lighting, and podium placement.

One reason why the candidates devoted so much attention to the details of the arrangements was previous experience with such debates. Given the importance of these events, neither candidate wanted to leave unattended any matter that might prove consequential. Another reason was that both candidates felt that League was extraneous to the process and that it understood neither practical politics nor the public interest. The candidates thus believed that the best way to guard against anything that might benefit one candidate over the other was to decide these particulars between themselves.

The most controversial aspect of the arrangements was the candidates' demand that they be able to exercise a right of approval over the selection of the panelists who would ask questions during the debate. This led a number of news organizations, including CBS, the *New York Times,* and the *Washington Post,* to announce that they would not participate in the process. The League initially submitted a list of twelve panelists for the candidates to consider, none of whom was accepted. It then presented a list of one hundred potential panelists to the two campaigns, but the two sides could agree on only three names from this list.[67] This response was vigorously denounced by the League, and its president, Dorothy Ridings, declared that "the process has been abused."[68] The controversy also fueled criticism of the League's handling of the process, with the most severe critics arguing that the organization had essentially abandoned its responsibilities and once again ceded control of the planning of these events to the candidates themselves.

This petty bickering, not to mention Reagan's double-digit lead in the polls, did little to diminish the public's interest in the debates. The first debate, which was limited to domestic policy and largely centered on economic issues, was watched by at least 85 million viewers.[69] Reagan principally argued that his administration's policies had produced a growing economy and that Mondale's plan to raise taxes would undermine this recovery. Mondale focused on the growing annual budget deficits as a sign of the administration's failure and charged that Reagan would have to increase taxes in his second term to reduce these deficits. The general postdebate consensus was that Mondale had been the more effective speaker and that Reagan appeared "tired, even at times confused."[70] Public opinion surveys confirmed the initial impression that Mondale had won,[71] and, in the days after the event, his campaign's internal polling showed that he had narrowed Reagan's lead from about 15 percent to 9 percent.[72]

But Mondale failed to gain further ground from the second debate, which was devoted to a discussion of defense strategy and foreign affairs. Prior to this affair, there was much speculation among the press as to whether Reagan would "recover" from his relatively poor showing in the first confrontation to exhibit the more poised and confident manner he had displayed in 1980. Journalists also wondered whether Mondale could provide another strong performance

and perhaps mount a major electoral upset. The candidates engaged
in a fairly substantive discussion of some of the major foreign policy
issues, but their views were overshadowed by the postdebate commentary on Reagan's performance. Most observers decided that
Reagan did well enough to call the debate a draw,[73] which, in their
view, was enough to guarantee his reelection.

Postelection analyses once again documented the effects of the
debates on voters' evaluations of the candidates.[74] A *Los Angeles Times*
survey revealed that just about 10 percent of the electorate cited the
debates as the basis for their voting decision. Of these, three out of
four voted for Mondale.[75] So while the debates had a major influence
on the dynamics of the race and helped Mondale revive his failing
campaign, their effect ultimately was not enough to change the predicted outcome, given the dimensions of Reagan's lead throughout
the campaign. But if the race had been as close as that of 1980, the
debates might have made the difference.

THE 1988 DEBATES

After the 1984 election, two national study groups issued reports on
the presidential debates process that led to a dramatic change in the
sponsorship of these events. The first analysis was conducted in 1985
by the Commission on National Elections, a bipartisan group sponsored by the Center for Strategic and International Studies at
Georgetown University, cochaired by Robert Strauss and Melvin Laird,
and comprised of forty respected leaders in the areas of public policy, business, labor, and media. The Commission included representatives of previous debate sponsors, the networks and the League of
Women Voters, and as part of its survey of a range of presidential
election issues disclosed a number of findings on candidate debates.
In its final report, the Commission noted that: (1) debates are an
integral and enhancing part of the process for selecting presidential
candidates; (2) American voters expect debates between the leading
candidates for president; and (3) debates among those candidates
should become institutionalized as part of the electoral process.[76]
With respect to the third point, the report specifically argued that the
best way to ensure debates for the future would be for the parties to
assume the responsibility for sponsoring these events and gain a commitment from their respective nominees to participate. It further
recommended that the two major-party organizations should establish

a formal mechanism to handle debate details and otherwise ensure "that presidential candidate joint appearances are made a permanent and integral part of the presidential election process."[77]

In December 1986, another study group was assembled at Harvard University's Institute of Politics. Sponsored by the Twentieth Century Fund and led by former Federal Communications Commission chairman Newton Minow, this group, comprising thirty participants and observers of past presidential debates, independently reached conclusions similar to those of the Commission on National Elections. In the report, *For Great Debates,* Minow and coauthor Clifford Sloan stated that "debates make an important contribution to the quality of presidential campaigns" and recommended that these forums become institutionalized in order to eliminate the quadrennial speculation as to whether they would happen, which the report regarded as simply a distraction from the more important issues in a presidential campaign.[78] This study went further than the Commission's report, however, in that it proposed that the best way to ensure debates would be for the two major parties "to jointly—and immediately—establish a not-for-profit, tax-exempt, bipartisan Presidential Debates Organization to plan and administer a series of presidential debates."[79] The report also said that this organization should form a broadly based citizen advisory committee to assist with its sponsorship activities.

In February 1987, Paul Kirk, then chairman of the Democratic National Committee, and Frank Fahrenkopf, his counterpart on the Republican National Committee, acted on these recommendations. Their work led to the establishment of the Commission on Presidential Debates, a private, tax-exempt, not-for-profit corporation, whose sole purpose is to "organize, manage, produce, publicize and support debates for the candidates for President of the United States."[80] The Commission was originally established with a board of directors, consisting of ten members including cochairs Kirk and Fahrenkopf, and a national advisory board of forty members. In accordance with its independent, nonprofit status, the Commission is not affiliated with any political party and is solely funded from private contributions; it receives no monies from the government or political party organizations. Nor does it report on elections, take positions, or lobby on public policy issues.

Once formed, the Commission quickly set about the task of preparing for the 1988 debates. As early as July 7, 1987, it announced that it would sponsor debates in 1988 on September 14 in Annapolis,

September 25 at Wake Forest University in Winston-Salem, October 11 in Pittsburgh, and October 27 in Omaha.[81] It was also just as quickly wrapped in controversy. The League of Women Voters resisted the notion of Commission sponsorship from the start, arguing that it would be a more impartial sponsor itself than a Commission led by the former heads of the two major parties. On July 1, 1988, it announced its own proposed schedule of debates, comparable to the Commission's, to be held on September 8 in Birmingham, October 6 in Minneapolis-St. Paul, October 23 in Boston, and November 1 in Los Angeles.[82]

The Commission also encountered resistance from the candidates. Even though for the first time in two decades there was no incumbent in the race to resist sharing the presidential aura, the Commission had problems similar to those experienced by the League in previous elections in getting the candidates to agree to its proposed schedule. The two major contenders, George Bush and Michael Dukakis, were locked in a tightly contested race by early September, with Bush having made up substantial ground after trailing by as much as 17 points in July. Both candidates felt a need to debate and believed the debates would play a decisive role in the election, but the Bush campaign in particular wanted them held on terms decided by the candidates, not the Commission. Bush's advisers also wanted to delay because they felt that the announcement of debates would "freeze" the campaign—that is, it would cause voters to wait until the debates to make further decisions about whom to support—and they wanted to maintain their campaign's momentum.[83]

Consequently, representatives of the two candidates engaged in a prolonged negotiation over details and format. The Dukakis campaign sought four debates, three presidential and one vice presidential, and direct exchanges between the candidates in addition to what had become the standard format of questioning by a panel of journalists. The Bush campaign, however, initially offered to participate in only one presidential debate and thereafter refused to budge from the arrangement used in 1984, which called for two presidential and one vice presidential contests and no direct exchanges between the candidates. Ultimately, the Dukakis campaign acceded to Bush's preferences and agreed to the two-and-one format, with presidential debates on September 25 and October 13 and a vice presidential debate on October 5. Two of the forums were to be sponsored by the Commission on Presidential Debates and one by the League of Women

Voters. The campaigns also sparred over a myriad of other details, such as the length of the sessions, panel selection, stage set and lighting, camera shot limitations, types of microphones, height of the podiums, and even the use of dressing rooms. All of these details were outlined in a sixteen-page "Memorandum of Understanding" presented to the sponsors as a set of mandatory conditions for the candidates' participation.[84]

The Commission accepted the candidates' demands and went about the task of planning its debates. The League, however, argued against these stipulations, which it described in a press release as "a closed-door masterpiece."[85] In particular, it expressed concern about the lack of follow-up questions by the panelists, the open-ended financial responsibility it had to assume to stage the debates, and other candidate specifications, such as the particular backdrop and rugs to be used in the staging. Accordingly, on October 3, League president Nancy Neuman announced that it was withdrawing its offer to sponsor the debates on the principle that the campaigns were taking control of the events. Thus, all three debates were sponsored by the Commission on Presidential Debates.

As in 1984, the squabbles surrounding the debates apparently did little to dampen the public's interest in them. According to the Commission on Presidential Debates, an estimated 160 million Americans watched at least one. Nielsen ratings also indicated a sizable audience and estimated that 58 percent of television viewers watched the second presidential debate.[86]

The first presidential debate, held at Wake Forest University on September 25, drew mixed commentary. In this encounter, the candidates essentially continued the arguments that had come to characterize the campaign, with Bush attacking Dukakis for being "too liberal" and for having vetoed a bill approved by the Massachusetts legislature that would have required teachers to lead their class in reciting the Pledge of Allegiance. Dukakis countered these assaults by accusing Bush of failing to handle the drug problem and by questioning the qualifications of his running mate, Dan Quayle. The candidates also aired their differences on the Reagan administration's defense buildup, the role of the government in providing health insurance, and the morality of the death penalty.

Some observers thought Dukakis had been more effective, others Bush, but many considered the debate a draw, with Dukakis outdistancing Bush "on points" and Bush projecting a better "image."[87] Some observers expressed disappointment, claiming that the event had simply served as another setting for the candidates to attack each other and air predetermined sound bites rather than provide the public with a reasoned discussion of the issues facing the nation. Veteran journalist Walter Cronkite characterized the debate as "phony, part of an unconscionable fraud,"[88] and columnist George Will called it "a national embarrassment."[89] Others disagreed, describing the debate as "surprisingly substantive," and noting that the debate had allowed the public to gain a sense of the differences between the two candidates.[90] Public opinion seemed to reflect these divisions; most polls showed that the public was fairly evenly divided as to who won the debate, with Dukakis generally holding a slight edge.[91]

In a marked departure from previous elections, many observers considered the vice presidential debate to be important in 1988 because of the controversy surrounding Bush's selection of Indiana senator Dan Quayle as his running mate. Quayle was an unexpected choice for the number-two spot, and from the time of his selection he was forced to confront questions raised by his military record and relative lack of experience, especially as compared to Lloyd Bentsen, the Democratic nominee, who had been a presidential candidate previously and was a well-regarded leader in the U.S. Senate. Dukakis's campaign manager, Susan Estrich, referred to the vice presidential meeting as "the second presidential debate" and hoped that the debate would encourage further questions about Quayle's experience, thereby causing voters to question Bush's judgment.[92]

Quayle's lack of seasoning was indeed raised in the debate, and on three separate occasions panelists asked questions about his preparedness to serve as president. On the last such occasion, Quayle noted: "I have as much experience in the Congress as Jack Kennedy did when he sought the presidency." To which Bentsen responded: "Senator, I served with Jack Kennedy. I knew Jack Kennedy. Jack Kennedy was a friend of mine. Senator, you're no Jack Kennedy."

Bentsen's comment later dominated the news coverage. Commentators unequivocally declared that Bentsen had bested his opponent, a view that was shared by a vast majority of the public, according to opinion polls.[93] Yet although Bentsen's statement was aired repeatedly in the following days, the vice presidential confrontation apparently had little effect on the overall voting. The polls did show a small increase in Dukakis's support in the days after the debate, but this rise proved temporary and Bush retained his lead entering the second presidential round.

The second presidential debate, held on October 13 in Los Angeles, was described by one observer as "more of the same."[94] Another analysis said this forum "was much less enlightening than the first, and covered much of the same substantive ground (including the issues of taxation, abortion, and capital punishment)."[95] The key issue for many commentators, however, was not substance but the images portrayed by the candidates. Many argued before the debate that Dukakis had to demonstrate more personality in order to address his "ice man" image.[96] The focus of news program chatter thus became Dukakis's response to a question by CNN anchor Bernard Shaw.

Shaw apparently hoped to give Dukakis an opportunity to address this image question in the debate. He asked Dukakis if he would favor an "irrevocable death penalty" if his wife were raped and murdered. The question was designed to draw an emotional response, but Dukakis replied by noting that he had "opposed the death penalty during all of my life," and went on to discuss how crime had been reduced in Massachusetts and the need to fight drug traffic. The lack of passion in his response led many reporters to accept this moment as a symbol of Dukakis's image problems, and the segment was widely aired and discussed in follow-up coverage.[97]

But the more important consequence of the exchange was to heighten criticism of the role of the press in the debate process. Many commentators argued that Shaw's question was a clear example of the problem of having journalists serve as panelists. They asserted that, instead of acting as public representatives and eliciting the type of information of greatest value to voters, journalists were improperly asserting themselves as participants in these events, asking biased or emotion-laden questions designed to trip up the candidates or produce a news story. Their participation thus served to undermine the educational value of these forums rather than enhance it.

Despite these problems, the debates continued to demonstrate their value. Although they did not change the minds of many voters in 1988, they did help to inform the public and made a substantial contribution to voters' understanding of the differences on issues between the candidates.[98] For example, a Times Mirror survey conducted on the weekend before election day found that almost half of the electorate judged the debates to be "very helpful" in deciding who to support.[99] Another study found that even with the press panel format, there was an extensive amount of direct confrontation and clash between the candidates, which helped to highlight the differences between the major-party nominees.[100]

Thus, by the end of the 1980s, there was a widespread consensus that debates had proved to be a valuable component of presidential election campaigns. This was certainly the view of the vast majority of the electorate, which continued to follow the debates closely and relied on them more and more for information about the candidates, even though their novelty had ended many years before. Candidates had also come to regard debates as an essential part of their campaigns and increasingly accepted them as a responsibility that could not be avoided without alienating a substantial portion of the electorate. While analysts throughout the 1980s pointed out a number of problems with formats and sharply criticized their press coverage, few argued against the need to make these events a permanent feature of the presidential selection process. Instead, most offered suggestions as to how to improve the candidate forums so that they would be an even more effective vehicle for educating the electorate. In the years preceding the 1992 vote, the major issue was no longer whether there would be debates but whether changes would be made to correct the problems raised earlier. It is safe to say that no election watcher expected to see some of the changes that actually took place.

Chapter Two

The 1992 General Election Debates

The 1992 debates were by far the most innovative and interesting of any recent general election campaign. For the first time, three candidates shared a single stage. The issues were discussed in four different formats, including the first use of a single moderator and a "town hall meeting" style. All four debates were held during a nine-day period, turning them into a televised "miniseries" that attracted a wide viewership, including the largest audience ever to watch a presidential debate. The use of varied formats in a condensed period of time close to the election provided voters with invaluable information about the presidential hopefuls, and, according to one postelection survey, almost three-quarters of the electorate found them helpful in deciding how to vote.

Although the debates were ultimately successful, their success was by no means certain when planning began. The road to the debates was littered with false starts, sponsorship and format disputes, and political posturing by the major party candidates, which undermined the promise of these events. Despite the continuing efforts of the Commission on Presidential Debates, the general election campaign began with no agreement among the candidates on the issue. As late as mid-September, the candidates had still not reached a consensus on the number of appearances and format, or, for that matter, whether they would debate at all. Some observers even began to predict that debates would not be held, their speculations fueled by vague statements suggesting as much from the Bush campaign in the last week of September. So, for the fifth consecutive election cycle, debates were staged, but the process that led to their production raised vexing questions about how to guarantee these events in the future.

Preliminary Proposals

After the 1988 election, the board of directors of the Commission on Presidential Debates decided to build on its initial experience as a debate sponsor by conducting an in-depth study of the effectiveness of different debate formats in an effort to determine which would yield the best possible information to the electorate. The Commission held a symposium in May 1990 that brought together 125 academic experts, journalists, pollsters, and campaign representatives to review the 1988 debates and consider alternatives for the future.[1] The group also sponsored research on past debates, including forums held during the primary campaigns, to assess the information content of various formats and sponsored a videotaped program of interviews conducted by Jim Lehrer of the *MacNeil/Lehrer NewsHour* with former presidents Ford, Carter, and Reagan, and former vice president Mondale and ex-representative Ferraro, who shared their thoughts on format and other matters.[2]

Upon reviewing the findings of this research, the Commission's board unanimously agreed to recommend for 1992 four ninety-minute debates—three presidential and one vice presidential—all to be conducted by a single moderator. The rationale behind this proposal, as explained by Commission cochair Frank Fahrenkopf,

> was simply that the focus of debates should be on the candidates, not any other participants. . . . Each additional individual who participates in a debate as a panelist reduces the time devoted to the candidates' views. We believed that a single moderator would best be able to elicit substantive responses and rebuttals from the candidates, thereby giving viewers and listeners the most information about their positions, personalities, and capabilities.[3]

The Commission was also concerned about the scheduling of debates, given the complicated network broadcast commitments in the months of September and October (particularly, the large number of sporting events that are added to regular programming). Accordingly, Fahrenkopf and his fellow cochair Paul Kirk began talks with network executives in February 1991 "to identify which nights would be best to avoid any major conflicts."[4]

The major networks also engaged in an effort to improve the debate process, independently of the work being done by the Commission. Citing the widespread criticism of the content of the 1988 debates, the presidents of ABC News, CBS News, NBC News, and CNN worked together in 1991 to develop a debate plan that would maximize viewership and enhance the information available to voters. "We're trying to erase some of the errors of the 1988 campaign and earlier campaigns that produced debates that really weren't debates," said Lane Venardos, the CBS vice president for hard news and special events.[5] The network officials sought to avoid the problems already noted by the Commission, such as the lack of interaction between the candidates and conflicts with broadcast schedules. To that end, they issued a proposal on September 24, 1991, that closely followed the Commission's earlier recommendations. It called for an end to the press panel format that had characterized most debates since 1960. In its place, the networks offered the resources needed to produce four ninety-minute, prime-time debates—three presidential and one vice presidential—to be conducted by a single moderator and held between September 15 and October 15. They offered the anchors of their respective evening news broadcasts to serve as moderators and vetted their schedules to avoid conflicts with major events and give no advantage to any particular network. The debates would be held on the four most-watched weekday nights and would be broadcast from studios in New York, Atlanta, Chicago, and Los Angeles with no live audience.[6]

A major objective of the network proposal was to avoid the prolonged negotiations between candidate organizations that have been a staple of the debate process since 1976. By settling on a format well in advance, the networks hoped at least to reduce the amount of bargaining that took place during the general election campaign.[7] In addition, they felt their proposal's single-moderator format would "provide a fuller, more direct exchange among the candidates."[8] They also argued that this approach, by abolishing live audiences, would better serve the broader national audience since, as CBS political director Martin Plissner noted, "the on-site audiences in past years had turned into a partisan cheering section."[9] Among other advantages cited in support of the plan were the elimination of the need to solicit public sites or special funding for these events and the absence of a Sunday night debate, which could be particularly difficult to start on the hour due to the unpredictable nature of Sunday sports events. Upon its release, the League of Women Voters embraced the proposal, noting that it eliminated the press panel format that "allowed candidates to grandstand rather than answer hard questions, often before highly partisan audiences that cheered and jeered." The plan would thus be more likely to result in an "unscripted debate" that would be of great value to voters.[10]

The network proposal led to a brief negotiation between the broadcast executives and the Commission on Presidential Debates. Although the two sides agreed on the number of debates and a single-moderator format, they disagreed on other essential details. The Commission opposed the network suggestion on in-house moderators because of its desire to include Jim Lehrer of PBS as a potential participant, as well as representatives of other media, particularly print journalists.[11] They also preferred to hold the debates in public settings, such as colleges or historic sites, and wanted at least one debate on a Sunday evening instead of the four weeknights offered by the broadcasters.[12] Most important, the Commission argued that network sponsorship represented a potential conflict of interest that must be avoided. Cochairs Kirk and Fahrenkopf warned against "conflicts which arise when media organizations whose function it is to report political news undertake to produce or participate in newsmaking events."[13] This viewpoint was seconded by others. "Networks tend to be owned by business interests with high stakes in who wins an election," said executive director Janet Brown, "and, anyway, networks are supposed to cover the news, not help make it."[14] Such concerns were among the reasons why the Commission was formed in the first place,[15] and despite rejoinders by some news officials that the Commission also relied on business interests for its funding[16] and simply wanted to retain party control over the debates to avert possible embarassment for candidates,[17] the Commission maintained its position and rejected the networks' plan.

On June 11, 1992, the Commission released a proposal of its own that largely conformed to the preferences expressed in both its own study of various alternatives and in its response to the networks. The proposal called for four ninety-minute debates—three presidential and one vice presidential—with a single-moderator format. It recommended that the debates be held on four specific dates, which included one Sunday evening: September 22, October 4, and October 15 for the presidential debates, and September 29 for the vice presidential debate.[18] Around the same time, in anticipation of the likelihood of a major independent candidacy by Ross Perot, the Commission also announced its selection criteria under which third-party or independent candidates would be invited to participate. These standards, which were similar to those used in 1988, stated that candidate selection would be based on a review of several characteristics, including "(1) evidence of national organization; (2) signs of national newsworthiness and competitiveness; and (3) indicators of national enthusiasm or concern, to determine whether a candidate has a realistic chance of election."[19]

In issuing this proposal, the Commission's intent, explained Fahrenkopf, "was to start conversations with the campaigns early, in the hope that final arrangements could be made shortly after the conclusion of the nominating conventions."[20] The group assumed that the recommendation would serve as a starting point for negotiations between the Bush and Clinton campaigns, which were expected to begin after the national party conventions. As Fahrenkopf had written earlier in an letter to White House chief of staff Samuel Skinner, "the question as to whether debates will be held, how many, where, when, format, etc., is a matter that will not be finally resolved until the nominees and/or their representatives have an opportunity to meet and discuss same following the two nominating conventions."[21] In an effort to speed these deliberations and complete their proposal, the Commission announced on August 14 that it had selected four debate sites: East Lansing, Michigan; Louisville; San Diego; and Richmond.

THE DEBATE OVER DEBATES

The decision to debate and the specifics of debate logistics are a crucial component of modern presidential campaign strategy. The questions of how many forums will take place and under what conditions are issues driven by the political calculations of the respective candidates rather than the concerns of the public or debate sponsors. The amount of attention candidates devote to these issues reflects their awareness of the importance of debates and their understanding of the influence debates can have on voter opinion.

Historically, the individual challenging an incumbent president usually has been eager to debate, while the incumbent or a candidate enjoying a large lead in the polls has been more reticent about engaging his opponent on national television. It was therefore not surprising that the Clinton campaign readily accepted the Commission's proposal to debate after Bill Clinton received the Democratic Party's presidential nomination in July. The Bush campaign, however, was not so eager to place the president on the same stage with his challenger. Although the president and his strategists acknowledged that there would be debates, they hoped to exert as much influence as possible over any final plan.[22] As a result, the electorate was forced to endure more than a month of political maneuvering and negotiations by the two major-party campaigns before the 1992 debates became a reality.

On September 3, the Bush campaign formally rejected the Commission's proposal, citing specific concerns about the number and format of the debates. It indicated a preference for the approach employed in 1988, with only two presidential meetings and use of a press panel, questions-and-answers format.[23] Bush's staff also advanced another justification for its decision: the question of the legitimacy of the Commission's role as debate sponsor. "Our understanding," said Bobby Burchfield, the Bush campaign's general counsel, "was that the [Commission on Presidential Debates] held itself out primarily as one of many potential sponsors for the debates, that it claimed no mandate from either political party or any candidate in 1992, and that it would not insist or advocate any specific schedule or format for the 1992 presidential debates."[24] This position was further explained by Bob Teeter, Bush's campaign chairman, in a letter sent to Clinton campaign chairman Mickey Kantor, inviting discussions of debates.

> We strongly believe that in the General Election Campaign the candidates themselves should determine the criteria upon which they debate and then seek a sponsor who will agree to the terms and conditions of the candidates. No one organization or group should be able to arrogate unto itself the authority to unilaterally make decisions that can be so critical to the final election result. A considerable amount of time and effort has gone into arriving at these debate terms [used in prior presidential debates] by good Democrats and Republicans over a period of sixteen years.[25]

The Clinton campaign initially rejected the Republican view, arguing that the Commission plan "presents a level playing field for the candidates to present their views. . . . As a result, we do not believe that any 'behind-closed-doors' negotiations between the campaigns are necessary." Moreover, said Kantor, "to the extent that any details need discussion, we believe that the discussions are properly held under the auspices of the Commission."[26]

This initial sparring produced a deadlock in negotiations and a period of charge and countercharge, which eventually forced the Commission to cancel the first proposed debate. Clinton took full advantage of the lack of an agreement, claiming that the president was "hiding" from the debates for fear that he would have to defend his economic record. His campaign also highlighted Bush's refusal to work with the Commission by having Clinton appear at a "debate day" rally in East Lansing, and later in Louisville, on the dates recommended by the nonpartisan organization for the first two meetings. The Democrats also encouraged volunteers to appear at Bush's campaign stops in chicken outfits to draw attention to "Chicken George's" unwillingness to agree to a schedule.[27]

Throughout September, the Commission kept up its efforts to advance the debate process. The organization continued to emphasize its willingness to work with the two candidates to reach a final agreement. After the first debate was canceled, the Commission offered to meet with the respective campaign chairs to discuss a revised schedule that called for the conversion of the September 29 vice presidential forum into the first presidential debate, a vice presidential debate on October 4, and a final presidential debate in Richmond on October 15. While the Clinton camp was willing to meet, Bush's camp continued to hold out.[28] After the second proposed debate in Louisville had to be canceled, Commission cochair Kirk (the former Democratic Party chair) declared, "I don't think George Bush feels that debates are in his best interest. That's the political bottom line."[29]

Despite this public pressure and a double-digit Clinton lead in the polls, the Bush campaign refused to begin debate discussions in September. Bush campaign officials continued to voice their opposition to any three-debate, single-moderator plan or Commission participation in negotiations. Bush's strategists believed that the proposed format was not in their candidate's best interest. They were particularly concerned about the single-moderator format since they felt it would have the effect the Commission intended—to promote more direct interaction between the candidates and facilitate follow-up questions. Reportedly, Bush campaign officials argued against the single moderator by noting that the panel format would allow Bush to appear "more presidential" because it would "be less likely to prompt a head-to-head rhetorical fight."[30] In addition, they feared that the single moderator was better suited to Clinton's style and "might subject the President to follow-up questions on issues that he is not comfortable discussing at length."[31]

The Bush campaign was also concerned about the broader strategic consequences of debates. Former secretary of state James Baker, who had stepped down from his position to oversee Bush's general election effort, felt that an early debate agreement would hinder the president's effort to make up ground on his challenger. Baker's view was said to be that Clinton had more to gain from debates than the president since the debates would help close "the stature gap" between the president and the Democratic nominee. Further, Baker claimed that the scheduling of debates would tend "to 'freeze' the campaign in place, essentially putting the candidates on hold until the debate occurs."[32]

Bush, however, failed to narrow Clinton's lead. Instead, the "debate debate" led to a widespread public perception that Bush was stalling the process, which encouraged Clinton to sharpen his attacks.[33] A *New York Times*/CBS News poll taken just after Labor Day found that 63 percent of registered voters had the impression that Bush was avoiding debates.[34] A later *Time*/CNN/Yankelovich survey found that 46 percent of the public believed only Clinton wanted to debate, as opposed to 21 percent who thought both candidates wanted to debate and only 3 percent who perceived Bush as the sole willing candidate.[35] Focus groups conducted by the Clinton campaign also revealed discontent over Bush's tactics, with participants viewing his stand "as a reluctance to get into a discussion on jobs and private sector growth."[36] Focus groups sponsored by the Commission on Presidential Debates also found that the electorate was following the debate over debates and took a candidate's willingness to debate as a means of gaining insight into his character and strategies.[37]

The findings of these polls are noteworthy because they reveal the strength of the public's desire to see the candidates debate. Thus, although press coverage of the "debate debate" in past elections had been severely criticized as detracting from the substantive issues, it appears that such coverage does provide voters with information that helps them judge the campaign. Moreover, in 1992, it played a significant role in fostering an agreement between the candidates to debate.

Still facing a double-digit deficit in the polls, and mounting editorial and public criticism for his refusal to debate, Bush tried to "shake up" the race on September 29 by announcing his desire to meet Clinton on four consecutive Sunday evenings from October 11 to November 1, with two of the forums employing a press panel format and two others a single moderator.[38] This tactic broke the deadlock between the candidates and led the Clinton campaign to agree to face-to-face negotiations, without direct participation by the Commission, on September 30. Thereafter events moved quickly.

Following only two days of negotiations, the campaign representatives agreed to a schedule and formats late on October 2, and then drafted a thirty-seven-page written agreement outlining the terms and conditions governing the debates that was submitted to the Commission on Presidential Debates on October 5.[39] The proposed program called for four debates, three presidential and one vice presidential, each ninety minutes long, to be held between October 11 and October 19 and sponsored by the Commission on Presidential Debates. Each presidential matchup would be held under a different format: the first on October 11 would use a press panel format, with a moderator and three journalists asking questions; the second on October 15 would be a town-meeting type of forum, with a single moderator and live audience questions; and the third on October 19 would be split into two parts, with the first half featuring a single moderator and the second half a panel of journalists. The lone vice presidential meeting on October 13 would use a single moderator, with free-form discussion among the participants allowed. Both campaigns also agreed to invite Ross Perot (and his running mate, retired admiral James Stockdale) to participate in the debates. Perot had announced his decision to reenter the race during the negotiations, and neither campaign wanted to risk offending his supporters by making an issue of his participation.

Besides guaranteeing the first appearance of an independent candidate with the two major-party nominees in a nationally televised forum, the most innovative aspect of the agreement was the decision to stage a town meeting with a live audience of undecided voters posing questions to the candidates. This format was suggested by Clinton, who had participated in a large number of town meetings throughout the primaries and felt comfortable with this approach.[40] The Clinton negotiators doubted that their opponent would accept this proposal because they felt it favored their man. But the Bush negotiators did agree. Since his first presidential bid in 1979, Bush had held occasional "Ask George Bush" forums in which members of the audience asked him questions. "Bush liked the format," explained Bobby Burchfield, "and had historically performed very well in it."[41] Moreover, both campaigns recognized the popularity of "call-in" shows during the 1992 campaign and believed it "indicated considerable potential public interest and support for such a format."[42]

The Commission quickly accepted the candidates' proposal and agreed to sponsor the debates, despite a controversial provision that allowed the two campaigns to retain the option of striking journalists whom they considered unfair or unfriendly from the list of potential panel participants.[43] The Commission did express concern, however, about the requirement that Perot be included since it had not yet decided whether he met the criteria established for minor-party candidate participation. To this end, the Commission asked its advisory panel, chaired by Richard Neustadt of Harvard, to evaluate Perot's participation. Even though at the time Perot was below 10 percent in the major polls and was given no hope of winning the race by political experts and media commentators, the panel determined that he had a "remote, but real, more than theoretical chance" of pulling off a shocking surprise and met the standards of national significance.[44] On October 7, the Commission issued a letter inviting Perot to participate.[45] Meanwhile, on October 6, Perot and Stockdale had already accepted the campaigns' invitation to join the two major-party nominees. For the first time in broadcast history, the electorate would get to see a nationally televised face-off among three general election candidates for the Oval Office.

THE 1992 DEBATES: AUDIENCE AND EFFECTS

The 1992 debates generated extraordinary public interest. In fact, Ed Fouhy, who produced the debates for the Commission, declared that "more people watched the televised presidential debates in 1992 than any other political event in American history."[46] Even though only two of the forums began in prime time and the first debate was not broadcast by CBS due to a conflict with the baseball playoffs, audiences were 20 percent larger than those in 1988. And the viewership grew over the course of the presidential meetings, contrasting with the declines experienced in 1984 and 1988. The first presidential debate was watched by an estimated 81 million viewers, the largest debate audience since the sole Carter-Reagan meeting in 1980.[47] The second and third debates were seen respectively by an estimated 90 and 99 million viewers.[48] About 76 million tuned in to the vice presidential debate, an improvement of 8 million over 1988.[49]

The substantial interest exhibited in the debates can be attributed to a number of causes. Certainly, the inclusion of Perot intrigued the viewing public, especially given his late reentry into the race. The debates were held during a period when public attention was focused on the race, in a year when the electorate was following events particularly closely. Innovation was also very important. In her study of the 1992 election, Kathleen Hall Jamieson, one of the nation's leading experts on broadcast debates, found that "a reason we had such high voter viewership of debates this year was the variability in the format." In addition, "voters were intrigued by the idea in the Richmond format [that] they would be able to participate through surrogates."[50] The tight grouping of the debates may also have promoted large audiences since it helped create a "miniseries" effect that encouraged viewers to watch the next episode.[51]

Increased public interest was also a result of the quality of the debates. There were "none of the serious 'gaffes' and few of the often seemingly rehearsed one-line retorts which frequently attracted media attention in past debates."[52] Although some observers continued to cast the debates as "nondebates" because the formats did not allow the candidates to cross-examine each other or permit open-ended discussion,[53] a majority of the electorate found them to be meaningful and informative. While Bush did stress concerns about Clinton's trustworthiness and character, the candidates did not engage in the sort of sustained attacks or posturing that marred the 1988 election. Instead, much of the discussion focused on the economy, budget deficit, and the candidates' respective policy proposals.

To a certain extent, the richer content of the debates was a function of candidate strategies. Clinton entered the fray hoping to convince the electorate of the need for change by concentrating on the nation's economic problems and the failure of previous Republican administrations. As George Stephanopoulos, Clinton's communication director, explained, the strategy was "really very simple. Answer the question—and then talk about the economy."[54] Perot, too, sought to focus on the issues, especially the federal budget deficit. At the start of the first debate, Perot answered a question about his relevant experience for the nation's highest office by declaring, "I don't have any experience in running up a 4 trillion dollar debt." Throughout the debates he mentioned the deficit repeatedly as he answered questions about his proposed gas tax and other deficit-cutting measures.

Voters also benefited from the multiple formats, which included questioning by professional journalists as well as members of the public. Prior to the debates there was some question as to the value of having "average citizens" ask questions of the candidates. Critics argued that the resulting broad questions would allow the candidates to give standard or rehearsed responses; ordinary folk, they claimed, lack the expertise needed to raise incisive questions that would challenge the candidates to move beyond canned replies. As Helen Thomas of UPI, one of the panelists for the third debate, observed, "A reporter, if given the chance, can try to pin the candidate down."[55] Others supported citizen participation as more relevant, claiming that journalists tend to raise issues that often are not of central concern to voters.

The moderator and panel participants in the first and third presidential forums did indeed tend to ask more detailed questions designed to elicit specific information on particular issues. These included queries about inconsistencies in statements made by the candidates, as well as explorations of national issues that had received little attention on the stump. For example:[56]

♦   Governor Clinton, can you lock in a level here tonight on where middle-income families can be guaranteed a tax cut, or at the very least, at what income level they can be guaranteed no tax increase?

♦   Mr. Perot, in the postwar cold war [sic] environment what should be the overriding U.S. national interest? And what can the United States do—and what can it afford to do—to defend that national interest?

♦   Mr. President, you keep saying that you made a mistake in agreeing to a tax increase to get the 1990 budget deal with Congress. . . . If you had it to do all over again, sir, which of those alternatives would you choose?

◆   Now there are rumblings that a commercial bank crisis is on the
     horizon. Is there such a problem, sir? If so, how bad is it and
     what will it cost to clean it up?

◆   Everyone wants a safe and clean environment, but there's an
     ongoing conflict between environmental protection and the
     need for economic growth and jobs. . . . [H]ow do you resolve
     this conflict between protection of the environment and
     growth in jobs, and why has it taken so long to deal with basic
     problems, such as toxic waste dumps, clean air and clean
     water?

In contrast, the town-meeting format used in Richmond was
designed to elicit the questions foremost in the minds of undecided
voters. Those who participated did tend to ask general and sometimes vague questions, yet they solicited the candidates' views on the
kinds of issues relevant to their own lives. For example, some of the
queries put to the candidates included:

◆   [C]rime is rampant in our cities. And in the Richmond area,
     and I'm sure it's happening elsewhere, 12-year-olds are carrying
     guns to school. . . . Where do you stand on gun control and what
     do you plan to do about it?

◆   What are your plans to improve the physical infrastructure of
     our nation, which includes the water system, the sewer system,
     our transportation systems, etc.?

◆   Please state your position on term limits, and if you are in favor
     of them how will you get them enacted?

◆   [Y]ou've talked a lot tonight about creating jobs, but we have an
     awful lot of high school graduates who don't know how to read
     a ruler, who cannot fill out an application for a job. How can we
     create high-paying jobs with the education system we have, and
     what would you do to change it?

◆   Mr. Perot, . . . what makes you think that you're going to be able
     to get the Democrats and Republicans together any better than
     these guys?

While some observers complained that these questions were "softballs" that provoked "little actual debate,"[57] most judged them to be fairly reflective of voter concerns. Mickey Kantor preferred the format because "it gets over the filter that people in the media and, frankly, people in politics get into—the questions are more substantive."[58] Even members of the media acknowledged the value of the Richmond approach, including CBS anchorman Dan Rather, who decided that the town hall format "worked best because the questions were by far the best."[59]

Indeed, one of the defining moments in the debates came in response to a citizen's question. A young woman asked the candidates, "How has the national debt personally affected each of your lives? And if it hasn't, how can you honestly find a cure for the economic problems of the common people if you have no experience in what's ailing them?" Bush appeared somewhat perplexed by the question. He began his response by noting that the national debt affects "everybody" and mentioned interest rates. The young woman quickly intervened with the retort "How?"—giving the impression that the president was not addressing her question. Bush tried to start again, and then asked for clarification of the question, admitting, "I'm not sure I get it. Help me with the question and I'll try to answer it." The young woman rephrased her query, noting that she had "personal problems with the national debt." At this point, the moderator, Carole Simpson of ABC News, stepped in and offered, "I think she means more the recession, the economic problems today the country faces rather than the deficit." Bush then redirected his response accordingly but the effort came too late. The damage had been done.

Bush's apparent confusion was perceived to be demonstrable proof that he was "out of touch" with the voters and did not relate to their problems. In fairness, Bush's hesitancy was understandable given the inexact language of the question. Clinton, having the benefit of speaking after Bush, understood the meaning of the question (he "got it") and seized the opportunity it afforded, walking over to the audience to address the woman directly and telling her that Arkansas was small enough that when people lose their jobs or a business goes bankrupt, there is "a good chance" that he, even as governor, would "know them by their names." These contrasting replies gave the electorate a valuable insight into the personalities of the two major contenders.

Perhaps the most unexpected aspect of citizen participation was the participants' eagerness to have genuine concerns addressed.

Throughout most of the campaign, the major controversy between Bush and Clinton centered on the issues of character, experience, taxation, and economic recovery. The first presidential debate began by focusing on these very issues. The participants in the town-meeting debate, however, sought to move beyond the strategic posturing on taxes, personal histories, and the like. One questioner declared that "the amount of time the candidates have spent on this campaign trashing their opponents' character and their programs is depressingly large." Another asked the candidates to "focus on the issues and not the personalities and the mud." These suggestions, quickly endorsed by Clinton and Perot, helped keep the discussion directed toward public problems and policy proposals, and steered it away from the candidates' prearranged attack strategies. These citizen representatives thus justified their inclusion in the process and promoted the public interest in the debates.

To cite the benefits of the 1992 formats is not to argue that the debates achieved their full potential as a means of providing information to voters. The candidates' agreement establishing the debates set forth clear "ground rules" that mitigated their potential impact. The terms prohibited follow-up questions in the first debate and for the panel portion of the third debate. They also prohibited candidate-to-candidate questioning and mandated short, one- or two-minute responses. These parameters discouraged direct confrontation between the candidates and limited the sessions' usefulness to voters.

The format that offered the greatest promise of back-and-forth exchanges and interaction between the candidates was the one used in the vice presidential meeting. It called for a single moderator and more free-flowing discussion among the participants. But, unfortunately, Vice President Quayle and Senator Al Gore chose to spend more time on character issues and attack strategies than on the problems facing the nation. As a result, the format proved to be more conducive to bickering than meaningful policy debate, which led Perot's running mate Stockdale, who was described in one report as being "no more than a bemused spectator,"[60] to confess at one point that he felt like "an observer at a ping-pong game."

Despite these drawbacks, the 1992 debates achieved their primary purpose, which was to make information available to the voters and help them in their voting decision. Public opinion, at least as reflected in published surveys, was very clear. The electorate liked the debates and found them more helpful and useful than those of four years earlier. According to a Times Mirror survey conducted after the election, 70 percent of the public said the debates were helpful in making their decision as to which candidate to support. In contrast, a comparable Times Mirror survey conducted on the weekend before the election four years earlier found that 48 percent of the electorate rated the debates as helpful in deciding who to support.[61]

The debates generally played a larger role in the decision-making of traditionally low-turnout voters than they did for more habitual voters. While 50 percent of all adults said the debates exerted an influence on their choice of candidates, that proportion was significantly higher for those under twenty-five years old (61 percent), blacks (56 percent), Hispanics (57 percent), lower-income citizens (56 percent), and those who did not finish high school (58 percent).[62] The Times Mirror survey also found that the debates made the greatest difference to voters under fifty years of age, "whose increased participation in the [election] resulted in higher voter turnout."[63] Eighty-one percent of voters under thirty rated the debates as helpful, as did 73 percent of voters ages thirty to forty-nine.[64]

As in previous elections, the debates also served to educate voters. They provided the public with the only opportunities to view the three major candidates on the same stage answering the same questions. They also focused public attention on a number of important national issues. Most significantly, the postdebate Times Mirror survey found that, following the debates, "for the first time politically dormant concern about the budget deficit had risen to the forefront of the voters' minds."[65]

With respect to the outcome of the election, the debates proved indispensable to Bill Clinton's victory, although Ross Perot received the greatest relative benefit from the three national forums. Clinton's performance throughout the debates received high marks. He impressed many observers with his command of the issues and focus on his message, especially his emphasis on the nation's economic problems. He appeared to be most comfortable with the formats, particularly the Richmond debate, in which he often stepped away from his stool and approached the audience to respond directly to questions. He also displayed his understanding of the dynamics of the town hall format by allowing his opponents to respond first on a majority of the questions so that he would have the last word in most of the segments.[66]

Perot also managed well in the debates. These nationally tele-cast forums gave him an opportunity to "reintroduce himself" to the electorate after his months-long departure from the race. As one ana-lyst commented, the debates "became a showcase for Perot," with some voters perceiving the events as "Perot's convention."[67] In the first debate, in particular, Perot's folksy manner and well-rehearsed one-liners captured public attention. Surveys conducted immediate-ly after the event by CBS and Gallup/CNN/*USA Today* showed that voters were impressed with his performance and thought he had won the debate.[68] Although Perot did not do as well in the subsequent meetings, by the end of the three debates he had restored the public's confidence in his ability to deal with the economy and was regarded as the most trustworthy of the three contenders.[69] More important, the percentage of the electorate expressing an intention to vote for Perot in November increased from an estimated 7 percent at the out-set of the debates to almost 20 percent after the final bout.[70]

In contrast, George Bush, who entered trailing Clinton by a sig-nificant margin, failed to make up much ground throughout the course of the debates. Although he criticized Clinton's youthful anti-war protests and tax policies in each of the first two debates, he did not, in the opinion of many reviewers, press the attack on either occa-sion. Generally, Bush's performance in the first two meetings was described as disengaged or "passive,"[71] perceptions that were no doubt fostered by repeated showings in newscasts of the president looking at his watch in the second debate. Bush was "more spirited"[72] in the third debate, but most commentators judged his effort as "too little, too late."[73] In fact, some three-way national surveys found the presi-dent slipping beneath 30 percent support for the first time in the campaign after the debates had concluded.[74]

Overall, Clinton's performance in the debates significantly influ-enced his success on election day. His efforts reinforced his voting support and allowed him to maintain a comfortable lead in the polls moving into the final weeks of the campaign.[75] Although his overall share of the vote did not change significantly during the two weeks surrounding the three candidate meetings, the Times Mirror post-election survey showed that 13 percent of the electorate had made up their minds during the debates, and those voters supported Clinton by a margin of 43 percent to Bush's 29 percent and Perot's 28 per-cent.[76] More generally, the debates helped convince millions of vot-ers of Clinton's suitability to serve as president and of his capacity to handle pressing national problems, especially the economy. They also afforded him an opportunity—his only one—to share a stage with the incumbent, confront the president directly, and answer the charges being made against his character. Reminiscent of 1980, the challenger finished ahead. The ultimate winner, however, was the American public, who came away from the debates better informed by virtue of seeing the candidates discuss the issues in a series of joint forums.

Each experience with nationally televised debates offers further testimony to the value of these events. Each also offers an opportunity to judge the effectiveness of various arrangements and to pursue further improvements. In both these regards, the 1992 debates were no exception. They were widely considered to be the most successful broadcast debates in history. They were especially popular with audiences and helped the vast majority of the public in deciding how to vote. Yet the debates failed to resolve some of the perennial questions about scheduling, format, and sponsorship. As a result, many analysts remain dissatisfied with the debate process and seek additional changes in hopes of producing more informative and lively forums in the future.

CHAPTER THREE

SCHEDULE AND FORMAT

I n 1992, most of the debate about debates centered on the issues of scheduling and format. Each of the actors involved in the process—the Commission, the networks, the Bush and Clinton campaigns, even academic researchers and journalists—expressed different preferences as to the scheduling of the debates and advanced different conceptions of the format that should be used. This situation was not a new experience. The thorniest issues with respect to the debates held in recent election cycles have always been those concerning the specific arrangements for these forums. How many should be held, and when? Who should be invited to participate? Who should ask the questions? How long should each candidate have to respond? Should the candidates ask questions of each other? Should there be a live audience?

Virtually every scholarly analysis or independent study of the debate process over the last fifteen years has argued that the public's needs are best met through a well-planned series of debates, usually consisting of at least three presidential encounters and one vice presidential forum.[1] Consequently, between 1980 and 1988, the debates were roundly condemned for failing to provide the public with adequate opportunities to assess the candidates. In 1980, the disagreement between President Jimmy Carter and Ronald Reagan on whether to participate in a three-way debate with Independent candidate John Anderson led to a debate between only Reagan and Anderson and one essentially winner-take-all debate between Carter

and Reagan shortly before election day. There was no meeting of the
vice presidential hopefuls. In 1984 and 1988 the electorate had more
of a chance to scrutinize the candidates, but each of these contests
featured only two presidential and one vice presidential debates. In
1984, all of the debates were held in a two-week span in mid-October.
In 1988 there were no joint candidate appearances in the last three
weeks of the campaign. Not since 1976 has there been four meetings—three presidential and one vice presidential—spread over a
monthlong period at the height of the campaign.[2]

The predominant format has been a joint appearance by the
candidates conducted by a moderator with a panel of journalists who
ask the questions. The candidates have generally been given a pre-
scribed time limit for responding to each question, ranging from one
to three minutes, with an additional minute or two to rebut an opponent's answer. The rules have also allowed a short closing statement
by each candidate and, in most instances, a short opening statement.[3]
This format has discouraged open argument between the candidates
and generally prohibited candidate-to-candidate questioning or other
procedures designed to promote direct confrontations.

Many academics and journalists have refused to call these forums
"debates," arguing that they were so tightly staged and choreographed
that they amounted to nothing more than "joint press conferences."
They contend that the press panel format stifles interaction and the
type of give-and-take discussion that might provide a clear contrast
between the candidates (thus proving most helpful to voters).[4] Other
commonly cited problems with the format include the reduced opportunity for the candidates to express their views because of the amount
of time taken up by the panelists' questions, and the shift away from a
focus on the candidates themselves to the interaction between the
candidates and the journalists asking the questions, particularly given
the tendency of some panelists to ask "gotcha" questions designed to
trip up a candidate or provoke an unrehearsed response.

The 1992 debates represented a great step forward in resolving
both of the major difficulties raised by previous debates. The voters
were not only treated to a series that included three presidential
forums and a meeting of the vice presidential candidates, but they
also had an opportunity to see the candidates in a variety of formats
that constituted a dramatic move away from sole reliance on press
panels. This mixture of formats drew generally high marks from both
the electorate and debate specialists. The debates covered a wide

range of topics, allowed viewers to judge the candidates in different settings, let them see how the candidates responded to different types of questions, and gave them an opportunity to witness their interactions with members of the public as well as members of the press. They also produced a noteworthy amount of contrast and confrontation among the contenders. It is therefore not surprising that so large a share of the electorate found them helpful in making a decision on election day.

Indeed, the 1992 experience confirms what debate experts have argued for some time: that a well-planned series of debates employing a variety of formats would best meet the informational needs of the public.[5] A series offers a candidate a number of chances to explain his or her positions on the issues, as well as time to offer opinions on a range of subjects. It offers the viewer an ample opportunity to assess their statements and to gain a more complete understanding of the candidates and the major issues in the race. It thus avoids the pitfalls of a lone debate, which places too much emphasis on a single performance and might result in a distorted perception of a candidate. A series is also to be preferred because it increases the likelihood that there will be a vice presidential debate. This is especially important since a debate usually provides voters with their only chance to evaluate those who might be a heartbeat away from the presidency on the basis of more than a sound bite.

Finally, a series permits the kind of innovation practiced in 1992, in that clearly the ability to use different formats is largely a function of the number of debates to be held. In fact, a series encourages innovation because the candidates, who are generally risk-averse, are more likely to agree to a change in format if they know there are to be a number of debates. That is, they are less likely to regard a new format as risky if used in one out of three or four events than if used in a sole debate or in one of two.

The 1992 debates thus constitute a better model than do those of prior elections. But the success of this approach should not lead to the conclusion that the 1992 setup should be accepted in its entirety as the way to conduct future debates. Rather, it should serve as a guideline for seeking further improvements in format and greater public participation in these vital events.

Although the 1992 forums were a vast improvement over those of previous elections, they were not without faults. Nor did they quell the arguments among academic experts and journalists about the arrangements that would best fulfill the broad objectives of debating. The fundamental purpose of a debate is to give the voters a chance to see the candidates side by side in a way that "generates the most useful information about their characters and their positions on issues, while permitting the public to compare them."[6] A debate should also encourage public participation by being scheduled in such a way as to attract the largest possible audience; anything less would undermine its potential impact. Because a debate is conducted for the public's benefit, it should also offer citizens some meaningful role in the proceedings, either by allowing them to select topics and questions or, more preferably, by allowing them to ask questions directly.

SCHEDULING

One issue raised by the 1992 experience concerns scheduling. The four debates were packed into a nine-day period. This timetable was apparently initiated by Harry Thomason, a friend of Bill Clinton's and a well-known television producer who participated in the debate negotiations on Clinton's behalf. Thomason felt that a compact schedule would have the effect of turning the debates into a television miniseries, which would engage the public and prompt viewers to watch subsequent episodes. This would counteract the trend of recent elections, in which viewership declined with each debate.[7] His thesis conformed to the practical constraints the campaign representatives were facing. Because the candidates did not begin negotiations until the end of September, there were only four weeks left until the election. The Clinton campaign refused to hold a debate during the last weeks of the campaign,[8] which left few possible dates available, especially given the number of days that would produce a conflict with the baseball playoffs or other major sporting events. If four debates were to be held, they necessarily had to be scheduled quite closely together.

While it is not clear that the argument about an audience being mesmerized by a tight schedule won the day, advocates of Thomason's view cited the larger audience for each subsequent debate as proof of the "miniseries effect."[9] Debate expert James Unger of American University argued that the compact schedule had the advantage of minimizing the influence of postdebate "spin doctors" in the process because it gave campaign officials and other public commentators little time to review the debates, discuss them on televised talk shows, and otherwise broadcast their interpretations. He concluded that "viewing [the debates] as a single play with four acts is probably a lot better than [seeing] four independent acts," implying that the rapid succession of encounters might assist viewers' comprehension by encouraging them to view the debates as a whole rather than as separate campaign events.[10]

Although the audience did grow during the course of the debates, the extent to which this increase was a function of timing is difficult to discern. The innovative schedule did engage the public, and the debates were held in a period when most of the electorate had their attention focused on the campaign. But Ross Perot's participation, the first use of the town hall meeting style, and the generally high level of interest in the election, which was evidenced by both the findings of public opinion polls and the increase in voter turnout, also may have affected audience size. Jim Lehrer, who was one of the moderators of the debates, felt that heightened voter interest more than format was the key to the size of the viewership. "I don't believe the formats had a thing in the world to do with the size of the audience for the debates. I think it had to do with the fact that people were interested in the election, they were interested in the candidates, they were interested in the issues."[11]

Still, regardless of the effect of a tight schedule on audience size, many knowledgeable observers argue that debates better serve the public interest if they are spread over a longer period. Generally, these specialists call for a series of debates over the course of four or five weeks, beginning in mid-September and ending in the middle of October. The proposal offered by the networks and the original plan supported by the Commission both suggested this approach. Spreading the debates over a longer period offers a number of potential advantages. A longer period helps reduce potential conflicts with other broadcast events by making more dates available for scheduling. With careful planning, conflicts that might induce one of the major networks to decide not to carry the debate can be avoided, and debates can be scheduled to start at 8 or 9 p.m. Eastern time, at the height of prime-time viewing, rather than at 7 p.m., as was the case for three of the four debates in 1992. Such a schedule would help guarantee the largest possible audience, in part by making it easier for those on the West Coast to watch the debates.[12]

Lengthening the timetable would also allow the debates to become more integrated into the campaign. While some practitioners argue that any debate tends to "freeze" the campaign for a few days because the candidates often stop traveling to prepare and the media focus their coverage on the "debate story," a tight block of debates seems more likely to disrupt the campaign. The 1992 schedule had this effect, according to Hal Bruno, because during the nine-day debate period "the whole campaign came to a stop."[13] Extending the timetable would facilitate campaigning between debates, allow candidates to follow up on their debate performances, and encourage those voters whose awareness was raised by the debates to develop a more complete knowledge of the candidates by paying attention to their actions on the stump. In addition, since the first debate would occur relatively early in the fall campaign and the last debate nearer the climax, the series would extend over a period likely to encompass changes in candidate tactics, shifts in the emphasis on particular issues, and other relevant developments. To some extent, the questions presented in the debates are likely to reflect these changes. Thus, each subsequent debate is likely to provide viewers with a certain amount of new information or a richer perspective, which may enhance their collective value as a tool for educating voters.

There is also some evidence that suggests that the public may prefer a less compact schedule. Focus groups conducted throughout the 1992 general election period by members of the Speech Communication Association, a professional academic organization, found that, although the public liked the compressed nature of the debates, there was strong sentiment in support of an earlier beginning to the series. Many of the participants felt that an early debate was needed to "set a tone" for the general election campaign and "start getting some information out there."[14] This research also suggests that voters would like the debates to begin earlier because they tend to rely mainly on the debates for their information about the candidates.

PRESS PANELS

One of the most important issues raised by the 1992 experience is whether the press panel format should be accepted as the standard model for future debates. In the past, the basic assumption governing debate arrangements was that journalists were the most appropriate people to ask questions in a presidential forum. This was based on the premise that journalists follow the campaign most closely and are therefore best suited to explore the details of statements made on the stump, as well as highlight any inconsistencies in a candidate's positions. As one former debate panelist, John Mashek of the *Boston Globe*, has noted:

> I think we're there [at the debates as panelists] because we cover the candidates. . . . We're familiar with what the issues are; we're familiar with how far the debate has gone on those issues. We're familiar with what questions the candidates have not answered at a given point in time. And we can, as surrogates for an informed citizenry, push those matters a little bit further.[15]

While acknowledging journalists' expertise, a number of campaign watchers have seriously questioned the press panel approach. These analysts argue that the use of journalists as panelists muddles the role of the press in the debate process. By serving as debate panelists, certain members of the press become participants in the process they are supposed to be covering. As such, they often seek to "make news" by encouraging a candidate to say something new or support a position that he or she had not taken previously. Consequently, as panelists they tend to ask questions designed to trip up a candidate, provoke an emotional response, or otherwise move a candidate away from his or her standard campaign message. Some critics point out further that in recent elections, those selected have not been chosen by random or been picked by their colleagues; instead they have been invited to participate only after passing muster with the candidates, who reserved the right to object to any reporter suggested as a panelist. Accordingly, a number of major news organizations, including CBS News and the *Washington Post*, have taken the position that their reporters should not serve as members of these panels.

Moreover, journalists do not always ask questions that are designed to elicit the sort of basic information about the candidates' positions that voters are often looking for. Nor do they always put forth questions worded in such a way as to clarify a candidate's previous statements or highlight the areas of agreement or disagreement between the candidates. Nor do they pursue issues or solicit information that would help voters understand how the candidates would act if elected president. Instead, many of the questions asked by these panelists are related to the campaign stories that have made the headlines. Perhaps they are designed to provoke a spontaneous response on the part of candidates, or they are worded to make a statement or express a personal view in the context of asking a question. Questions of this sort undermine the potential educational value of a debate since their intent is to move candidates away from their campaign messages, instead of providing the competing politicians with opportunities to articulate their basic views. Although journalists who track the race closely consider these views "old news," it can be counted on that a significant portion of the public watching a debate has not heard these positions and is tuning in in order to gain a better understanding of the platforms and philosophies of the presidential contenders.

There are many examples from recent debates that could be used to highlight these claims. Perhaps the best-known instance is Bernard Shaw's query to Michael Dukakis regarding his reaction to a hypothetical fatal attack on his wife. But consider some of these others advanced by journalists in recent presidential forums.[15]

♦   Governor [Dukakis], . . . the theme that keeps coming up about the way you govern is passionless, technocratic. . . . Passionless, technocratic, the smartest clerk in the world. Your critics maintain that in the 1960's your public passion was not the war in Vietnam or civil rights, but no-fault auto insurance. They say that in the 1970s you played virtually no role in the painful busing crisis in Boston. Given the fact that a President must sometimes lead by sheer inspiration and passion, we need to know if this is a fair portrait of your governing or is it a stereotype? If it isn't fair, give us an example of where you have had the passion and leadership that sometimes a President needs. (First Presidential Debate, 1988)

♦   I quote to you [Vice President Bush] this from Article Three of the 20th Amendment of the Constitution: "If at the time fixed for the beginning of the term of the President, the President-elect shall have died, the Vice President-elect shall become President," meaning if you are elected and die before Inauguration Day, automatically—automatically Dan Quayle would become the 41st President of the United States. What have you to say about that possibility? (Second Presidential Debate, 1988)

♦   Governor [Dukakis], you won the first debate on intellect but yet you lost it on heart. . . . The American public admires your performance but didn't seem to like you much. Now, Ronald Reagan has found his personal warmth to be a tremendous political asset. Do you think that a President has to be likable to be an effective leader? (Second Presidential Debate, 1988)

- Senator Quayle, in recent years the Reagan Administration has scaled back the activities of the Occupational Safety and Health Administration, prompted in part by Vice President Bush's Task Force on Regulatory Relief. The budget for the agency has been cut by 20 percent, and the number of inspections at manufacturing plants has been reduced by 33 percent. This has had a special effect in this area, where many people work in the meat packing industry, which has a far higher rate of serious injuries than almost any other [industry], a rate which appears to have been rising, although we're not really sure, because some of the larger companies have allegedly been falsifying the reports. Would you acknowledge to the hundreds of injured and maimed people in Nebraska, Iowa and elsewhere in the Midwest that in this case deregulation may have gone too far and the Government should reassert itself in protecting workers' rights? (Vice Presidential Debate, 1988)

- Mr. President [Bush], you keep saying that you made a mistake in agreeing to a tax increase to get the 1990 budget deal with Congress. But if you hadn't gotten that deal, you would have either had to get repeal of the Gramm-Rudman Deficit Control Act or cut defense spending drastically at a time when the country was building up for the Gulf War, and decimate domestic discretionary spending including such things as air traffic control. If you had it to do all over again, sir, which of those alternatives would you choose? (Third Presidential Debate, 1992)

- Mr. Perot, what proof do you have that Saddam Hussein was told that he could have the oil? Do you have any actual proof? Or are you asking for the papers? And also, I really came in with another question. What is this penchant you have to investigate everyone? Are those accusations correct? Investigating your staff, investigating the leaders of the grass-roots movement, investigating associates of your family? (Third Presidential Debate, 1992)

◆   Mr. President [Bush], why have you dropped so dramatically in
    the leadership polls from the high 80's to the 40's? And you have
    said that you will do anything you have to do to get reelected.
    What can you do in two weeks to win reelection? (Third Pres-
    idential Debate, 1992)

As these few examples suggest, reporters have at times been more
intrusive than instructive in fulfilling their responsibilities in the
debates. They have certainly not focused their questioning on the central policy issues facing the nation or on issues that would highlight the
differences between the candidates. This has led many analysts to conclude that journalists should not perform this function. Among them
is David Broder, the veteran columnist for the *Washington Post*, who
has said:

> I think the role of journalists in a political event of this
> size is much too intrusive. We ought to be covering the
> story, not participating in the story. I think the tempta-
> tion to dream up the question that is going to change his-
> tory is always there, and has occasionally been succumbed
> to. [For example,] those wonderful hypotheticals that are
> going to suddenly reveal the character of an individual.
> . . .[This] is a role, frankly, I don't think a journalist ought
> to play.[17]

Most observers share Broder's view and argue that the press
panel format should be replaced by some other approach, usually a
single moderator. Prior to the 1992 election, the Commission on
Presidential Debates, the broadcast networks, and the League of
Women Voters all supported debate proposals that would do just that.
Their consensus led to the use of a single-moderator format in the
1992 vice presidential debate and in the first part of the third presidential debate. The experience of these two encounters suggests that
a single moderator may in fact be a more effective and successful format than a press panel. With only a moderator asking questions and
guiding the discussion, there is more time available for the candidates to speak. There is a more natural flow of conversation and
smoother transitions from topic to topic, and the discussions are more
lively with better interaction among the participants. Furthermore, by
having a journalist or former reporter as moderator, the main

benefits attributed to a press panel, such as an expertise in asking questions and an informed understanding of the candidates and issues, are retained. The 1992 experience thus seems to endorse the single-moderator or some other format as a way to improve the quality of debates.

IMPROVING THE QUALITY OF INFORMATION

Focus group studies indicate that the public would prefer more informative debates that allow the candidates more time to answer the questions put to them. Many of the participants in these groups felt that the debates afforded no in-depth discussion of any particular issue. Instead, the strict time limits (one or two minutes) on answers forced the candidates to "sloganize their position" or "do the sound bite."[18] Such forced brevity does not allow the candidates leeway to discuss various aspects of complex issues or to rebut their opponent in a meaningful way (especially when specific time for rebuttals is not made available, which was the case in the 1992 debates). Future ground rules should be designed to address this problem in order to ensure that the debates provide voters with the new information they seek and a clearer understanding of the issues associated with a particular policy problem.

One means of promoting more detailed information would be to guarantee follow-up questioning by the moderator or other questioners in each debate. Follow-up questions can improve the informational value of a debate in a number of ways. For example, they enhance the ability of questioners to seek clarification of a candidate's position or to force a candidate to respond to a query more directly or completely. They can be used to solicit additional information and thus provoke a more in-depth discussion of a topic. They also invite a clearer contrast between the contenders by encouraging a candidate to rebut an opponent's view or to specify how his or her position compares to a statement made by an opponent. In spite of these advantages, fewer than half of the televised general election debates have featured follow-up questioning.[19] The most recent debates have made even less use of this practice, owing to the limitations imposed by the candidate agreements that set the formats. Formal follow-up questions were not permitted at all in the 1988 debates and were not allowed in the panelist portions of the first and fourth presidential debates in 1992 or in the vice presidential debate.

The problems that can arise from a lack of follow-up questioning have been described by Susan Rook of CNN, who served as a panelist in the 1992 debates.

> [D]uring the third presidential debate, the one that I was in, . . . [the lack of follow-up questions] was very constraining, especially when a candidate doesn't understand the question, like, for example, [when I was] asking then-President Bush about the issue of women and minorities getting beyond the glass ceiling, and he said, "Well, I have Margaret Tutwiler." And he just really didn't understand.
>
> I violated the format and jumped in and tried to correct him, which I shouldn't have done but couldn't help myself. . . . I would really urge to stop the ban on follow-ups because, if you just ask a question and it just goes floating out there, it doesn't do any good.[20]

An even greater concern has been raised by Kathleen Hall Jamieson, who argues that without formal follow-up questions, debates may actually be a source of misinformation. To demonstrate her point, she cites a statement made by George Bush's campaign press secretary, Peter Teeley, in 1984. "You can say anything you want during a debate," he observed, "and 80 million people see it." But when reporters demonstrate in postdebate articles that a candidate is misinformed: "So what? . . . Maybe 200 people read it, or 2,000 or 20,000."[21]

Others have suggested that the lack of follow-up questions may compel participants to ask complicated, time-consuming, multiple-part questions that can be difficult for the candidates to answer without resorting to general statements and may confuse the public. Or it may force panelists to repeat a question at different points in the debate in an effort to get a clear answer, as in the 1988 vice presidential debate, when Dan Quayle was asked three times what he would do as president.[22]

In fact, given the ambiguity and opacity of argument that might result from a lack of follow-up questioning, it is somewhat surprising that some candidates have opposed follow-ups. Presumably, those who objected felt that the greater scrutiny was not in their best interest. But follow-up questioning, as implied by Rook, can benefit the candidates. It serves as a tool for clarifying queries so that their specific wording does not cause a candidate to be perceived by viewers as confused or unresponsive. It also offers a candidate a second chance to respond to a query when he or she is not satisfied with an initial answer, as well as an opportunity to expound on a position or proposal.

Another way to improve the quality of the information provided by debates, while at the same time increasing the amount of time devoted to subjects critical to voter interest, would be to limit the scope of debate discussion. Instead of a format that permits questions on anything, as was the case in all of the 1992 debates, each debate might be devoted to a particular topic area or specific issues. For example, as in 1976, the first presidential debate could be confined to domestic policy issues, the second to foreign policy, and the third open to all questions. Since it is unlikely that there would be more than one vice presidential debate, it too would be open to any issue. (That such an approach is best suited to a schedule of at least three presidential debates stands as another reason for preferring a series of debates to one or two meetings.) This format has also been used to good effect in presidential primary debates. In 1992, Hal Bruno of ABC News moderated a very successful forum among the Democratic presidential hopefuls that was dedicated to a discussion of the economy and health care.

A bolder solution would be to adopt more innovative formats that provide the candidates with more time to explain their positions. One such format has been proposed by Kathleen Hall Jamieson and David Birdsell in their definitive study of modern broadcast debates. They suggest altering the traditional press panel format to include a modified version of the Lincoln-Douglas style of debate. Under this proposal, the first debate would consist of a single moderator and the candidates. Each candidate would open with an eight-minute statement, followed by six-minute segments for restatement and rebuttal and then two time slots of four minutes each for elaboration. The role of the moderator would be only to intervene and redirect the discussion if the candidates veered away from the topic established for the debate.[23]

While some may challenge the specific time periods suggested, the proposal has the merit of forcing the candidates to move beyond mere sound bites and rehearsed statements, thereby promoting a fuller discussion of the issues. This approach would eliminate the less focused discussion normally generated by the questions of press panelists and would dramatically increase the time available to the candidates to air their views. The content of the discussion would be determined by the candidates themselves, since the flow of debate would be dictated by the points raised in the opening statements and subsequent candidate responses. Accordingly, Jamieson and Birdsell argue that this approach, by eliminating the press panel, "would reduce the focus on the politics of the campaign and minimize as well the invitation to produce 'news.'" Further, it would clarify the role of the press in debates by removing "reporters from the story they are covering."[24]

Similar advantages might accrue from an "Oregon-style" debate. This format also would include only a moderator and the candidates. But instead of being based on lengthier candidate statements, it would emphasize direct confrontation between them. The candidates would each begin with an opening statement of perhaps five or six minutes. They would then ask questions of each other in rotation, with time allotted for rejoinder or rebuttal. Time limits would be set for each answer, but the amount should be no less than three or four minutes. The role of the moderator would be to monitor the proceedings and intervene only when necessary (for example, if a candidate is exceeding the time allowed for a response or if the candidates are talking at the same time).

Although this approach would involve smaller blocs of uninterrupted candidate speaking time, it might encourage more interaction between them and afford the public a better sense of the candidates' reasoning abilities, their comparative strengths in asking and answering direct questions, and their ability to defend their statements and policy proposals. Such an approach is also likely to be highly appealing to voters, who have continually expressed an interest in more direct confrontation between the candidates. In fact, this format was used with great success in the 1990 Massachusetts gubernatorial race between Republican William Weld and Democrat John Silber.

While a modified Lincoln-Douglas bout or Oregon-style forum offers great potential for educating the electorate, there are a number of cautions advanced by debate specialists that must be weighed in assessing these proposals. As Joel Swerdlow has noted, "people who advocate face-to-face confrontations may be expecting far too much from them."[25] There is no guarantee that either of these formats will produce more detailed or meaningful discussion. The candidates might still try to avoid uncomfortable questions or direct confrontation by giving evasive answers or by cluttering the discussion with unrelated points. Jamieson and Birdsell have acknowledged such risks.

> The risk in the Lincoln-Douglas form is twofold. By lengthening candidates' statements, the form limits the total number of responses by each. Conditioned by decades of television as entertainment, accustomed to rapid action and waves of visual stimuli, the marginally interested viewer might respond by fleeing to another channel. No intervening panel and moderator can ride herd on the candidate who transforms the debate into a series of set speeches.[26]

To compensate for the potential drawbacks, Jamieson and Birdsell suggest a series of meetings with mixed formats, including a conversational-style debate in which the candidates and a moderator would be seated around a table to provide open dialogue in a more informal setting. This variation has been used in a number of presidential primary debates with great success, although to date the general election candidates have dismissed it.

The success of any of these proposed alternative formats might largely depend on the effectiveness of the moderator in performing his or her role. Unless the chosen arbiter handles the candidates skillfully, instead of enlightened policy debate, the Lincoln-Douglas or Oregon styles might produce excessive confrontation, with lots of action and reaction but little clarity or detail. Candidate-to-candidate discussions could degenerate into "shooting matches" between the participants, or the sort of talking at cross-purposes or bickering that offers little help to the voter in making a choice.

An indication of the problems that might accompany more confrontational formats can be gleaned from the 1992 vice presidential debate, which did not mandate candidate cross-examination but did allow for a more free-flowing discussion. Early in this session, Vice President Quayle and Democratic senator Al Gore each attempted to dominate the discussion by making points without ceding the floor, which held out the threat of an unruly evening. Their actions compelled the moderator, Hal Bruno, to intervene, at first gently ("Thank you, Mr. Vice President. Admiral Stockdale, it's your turn to respond next, and then Senator Gore will have his chance to respond.") and then more forcefully ("Mr. Vice President, let him say

his thoughts and then you can come in." "The only thing I would ask
of you gentlemen . . . is that whoever talks first be considerate of the
others because you have a tendency to filibuster.") Bruno handled a
difficult situation well and managed to bring more order to the rest
of the proceedings, but it might not always be possible to have so
experienced a moderator at center stage to try to keep the debate
focused in a way that best suits the needs of the viewers at home.

PUBLIC PARTICIPATION

One final aspect of debate formats that must be given due consideration in light of the 1992 experience is that of public participation.
The success of the Richmond town hall meeting demonstrated the
popular appeal of citizen participation in these events. It also demonstrated the beneficial effects of such a format, as voters found the
event particularly meaningful and informative. According to Diana
Prentice Carlin, a leading academic authority who helped conduct
focus group studies on the debates in 1992, the viewers preferred the
Richmond format because the citizen-questioners raised issues that
the public wanted addressed and put forth questions in the manner
that people wanted them to be asked.[27] The public also preferred this
approach because it felt that the relationship between the voters and
the candidates made it more difficult for the politicians to evade their
questions than to duck a journalist's probe.[28] So, at least in the view of
focus group participants, this debate produced a real exchange
between the candidates and the voters.

The success of the Richmond debate suggests that other methods
of incorporating the public agenda should be considered. Although
the town meeting is currently popular, it may not remain so in the
future. The electorate may demand even further efforts to ensure
that its collective voice is recognized in the debates. This objective
could be achieved in a number of ways beyond a town hall forum.

One approach worth trying is to incorporate inquiries from the
public into the debates so that these better reflect the public agenda.
Given the wide availability of reliable, published polling data on the
issues of greatest concern to the electorate and the major themes in the
presidential race, it would not be difficult to develop a series of questions directed toward these concerns that could be asked during the
debates. These questions might be developed by an advisory panel
established by the Commission on Presidential Debates or by a group
of public opinion specialists sponsored by the Commission for this

express purpose. Another option might be to have the Commission solicit questions from members of the public. This could be done either by encouraging written submissions or by establishing an electronic bulletin board accessible through the major on-line services or other links available on the "information superhighway" or by making use of focus group studies done in advance of each debate for this purpose.

These questions would be selected by the Commission on Presidential Debates and asked by the moderator in the debates. To avoid reducing the moderator to nothing more than a talking head, these questions might be mixed with others that he or she initiated. Or questions suggested by the public could be followed up by queries from the moderator. The latter approach might prove to be particularly effective since it would help ensure that the candidates addressed the issues raised by voters. It might also help to reinforce the impression that the purpose of the debates is to facilitate an exchange between the voters and the candidates, and that they are held for the public's benefit. By enhancing public regard and expectations for the debates, this would make it even more difficult in the future for candidates to avoid the obligation to participate.

The public's role in the debates might also be expanded by inviting citizens who are not journalists to serve as questioners. For example, nationally known educators, business leaders, economists, foreign policy specialists, even members of Congress or other public servants might be included in debate panels. These individuals would bring different perspectives to the questioning and give less emphasis to questions designed to make news or catch the candidates off guard. As leaders in their respective fields, they would also add substance to the debates and might provoke the types of discussion that voters would find particularly helpful.

One current form of public participation that merits serious reconsideration, however, is the live studio audience. In recent years, the general election debates have been staged before live audiences composed of supporters of the candidates, political and civic leaders, and others invited by the debate sponsor. The debates thus provide a select group of citizens with an opportunity to be part of history, as well as a minor educational benefit in that they afford some insights that cannot be achieved by simply watching these sessions on television. But this advantage for a very small sampling of the citizenry does not outweigh the strong arguments advanced against live audiences. Critics complain that the audience serves little purpose in a debate other than as a distraction that may have an undue influence

on viewer perceptions and disrupt the flow of discussion.[29] This thinking informed the proposal made by the networks in 1992, which recommended that the debates be held in television studios with no live
audience. There is no doubt that in recent debates, audience reactions have briefly interfered with the discussion on numerous occasions, as boisterous members of the crowd have applauded, cheered,
laughed, gasped, and even hissed at comments made by the candidates. For example, in the 1992 vice presidential debate, there were at
least two dozen outbursts by the audience that interrupted the proceedings. As a result, Hal Bruno had to remind the audience a number of times about vocal disturbances and was forced to admit that
"trying to stop you [the audience] from applauding may be a lost
cause." At one point he even stated, "I do think [hissing] is discourte-
ous . . . and it reflects badly on the candidate you're supporting."[30]

Such reactions may color viewer perceptions. They may also influence candidate tactics by encouraging speakers to launch snappy one-
liners or witty retorts that might draw a favorable crowd reaction and
thus create the impression of an important moment in the debate.[31]
Although there have been no detailed studies of these effects, the
potential harm posed dictates that the need for a studio audience be
reconsidered.

Whatever judgments are made about the strengths and weaknesses of various alternatives, it is clear that the 1992 debates opened
the door to formats that move beyond the traditional press panel
approach. Despite the possible shortcomings of various proposals,
the arguments advanced in support of further innovation and more
informative debates are strong ones that merit consideration. The
best method of responding is to begin to experiment with new formats in primary campaigns or as part of a series of general election
debates. In the current political environment, it is likely that the candidates will continue to play an important role in the decisionmaking
associated with the debates. But if the experience of 1992 is taken as
a guide, it is likely that the candidates will be open to additional
changes. The most recent election demonstrated that there is ample
public interest in seeing the candidates appear in new formats. By
fulfilling the public's desires, the candidates can be assured of large
audiences for these events in the future.

CHAPTER FOUR

SPONSORSHIP AND CONTROL

As in 1988, the Commission on Presidential Debates sponsored the 1992 debates. This nonpartisan organization, whose sole purpose is to organize, produce, and publicize debates, efficiently and effectively produced all four 1992 forums, and did so under somewhat extraordinary circumstances. But the decision to have the Commission sponsor the events was not a foregone conclusion, and the particular events that framed this decision led some observers to question the group's efficacy and its value in future presidential elections.

The debate plan finally crafted by the Bush and Clinton campaigns called for four debates in nine days, an unprecedentedly tight timetable, considering the magnitude of these events. Furthermore, the candidates' plan was not finalized and submitted to the Commission until October 5, at which time the two campaigns, in accordance with the terms of their written agreement, formally invited the Commission to sponsor the debates. The Commission readily accepted the invitation and thus had only about a week to prepare for the first debate, which was to be held on October 11. During this period, it had to finalize site arrangements, select moderators and panelists, determine whether Ross Perot met its criteria for participation, and produce the debates.

That the Commission was able to fulfill its responsibilities in such a short time was largely due to its expertise. Building on its 1988 experience, the group was well prepared to handle the 1992 debates. The Commission had already identified potential debate sites around the country and had selected four host cities as part of its original debate proposal. Two of these locations, Louisville and San Diego, had to be changed as a result of the candidates' proposal, but they were quickly replaced with Atlanta and St. Louis.[1] The Commission had also prepared for the task of selecting moderators and panelists, and, for the second election cycle in a row, this was accomplished with a minimum of controversy and without extensive fighting between the presidential campaign organizations. Finally, the Commission had a process in place for determining whether a non-major-party candidate should be invited to debate. The organization had decided in September that candidates representing the New Alliance Party, Libertarian Party, and Natural Law Party would not be included in the debates since they had failed to meet its preestablished selection criteria.[2] Perot's reentry into the race once again raised the issue of candidate participation. But in response to the Bush and Clinton agreement, which invited Perot to participate, the Commission's advisory panel applied its standards to Perot's candidacy and within a few days issued its finding that Perot met the qualifications and would be included in all of the forums.

The Commission's performance led many participants to praise its actions and highlight the importance of its role in the debate process. Harold Ickes, who participated in the negotiations on Clinton's behalf, noted in testimony before a recent congressional hearing on presidential debates that the Commission "played an extraordinarily positive and useful role" in 1992. "I doubt that these debates would have been nearly as successful had the Commission not been there with its background, with its staff, with its expertise, with its contact with the media, having discussed with the media the myriad arrangements that are necessary [in] setting up a debate, picking the site, handling the tickets, handling the credentialing, setting the stage. All of those arrangements were extraordinarily helpful and contributed in great measure to the success of the debates."[3] Sander Vanocur, one of the panelists for the first presidential debate, said, "I would think that given the prestige bestowed upon the Commission by the way it discharged its responsibilities in 1992, it will be . . . in a stronger position than ever before to push its case that debates be debates, nothing more, nothing less, in 1996."[4] This perspective was shared by Newton Minow, former chair of the Federal Communications Commission and coauthor of the 1987 Twentieth Century Fund study that recommended the formation of an independent commission to serve as debate sponsor. "The accomplishments of 1992 have bolstered the stature of the Commission," he concluded, noting in particular the group's handling of the traditionally problematical issue of participation by an independent candidate. "The next time that Republican and Democratic candidates disagree over a third candidate's participation, the Commission's ruling [on Perot] will carry considerable weight with the press and the public."[5]

Other analysts were not as optimistic about the Commission's effectiveness. In fact, some felt that the 1992 experience, despite its successful outcome, demonstrated that the system was not working. Their primary contention was that the Commission did not play a meaningful role in the deliberations leading up to the debates. The Commission was created expressly to determine the terms of the debates and develop a proposal that would be accepted by the candidates. Its establishment was intended to eliminate the quadrennial "debate about debates" and to help ensure that the public's interests, not the candidates' political concerns or desires, would drive the debate process. Although the Commission did develop a plan well before the party conventions, it was not accepted by the party nominees. Instead, the debates were set only after prolonged maneuvering between the major candidates, which ended in a plan wholly designed by the candidates that was then presented for implementation by the Commission as a fait accompli.[6] Martin Plissner, the political director at CBS News, summarized the view of these critics when he declared, "Every aspect of the 1992 debates, as was the case in 1988, was decided by the candidates and delivered to the Commission on a take-it-or-leave-it basis. As in 1988, the Commission took it."[7] Susan Estrich, the manager of Michael Dukakis's 1988 campaign, concurred. "The one thing the League [of Women Voters] wasn't able to do, the Commission [also] wasn't able to do—and that's get both sides to put aside their political agenda and sign on the bottom line. It didn't work four years ago, and it'll probably never work."[8]

It is certainly true that the final decisions about the debates were made by the candidates. In this regard, the 1992 experience was typical; in fact, the pattern of recent elections has been that the candidates have tried to assume more and more control over the associated arrangements. In 1984, for example, the Reagan and Mondale campaigns negotiated a three-page agreement listing the conditions that would govern their debates; in 1988, the Bush and Dukakis campaigns negotiated a thirteen-page agreement; in 1992, the final agreement reached by the Bush and Clinton campaigns consisted of more than thirty pages of terms and conditions.[9]

The extent to which candidates have tried to control the debates is a reflection of their importance. Because these forums have proved to be so essential in shaping voter opinion, presidential aspirants resist planning by a third party, even when that party is an independent organization with no partisan interest. In general, candidates, especially incumbents or acknowledged front-runners, believe that direct negotiations with the opposition best serve their political interests; that is, they offer the best chance of securing terms that play to a leader's particular strengths. At the very least, such negotiations are less likely to result in arrangements that might expose the candidates to perceived "risks," such as free-flowing discussions or intensive cross-examination. This attitude towards debates has been especially pronounced among recent Republican candidates because, in practice, they fared well in both 1984 and 1988, gaining most of what they wanted in terms of the number of debates and format.[10]

Interestingly, the 1992 experience gives reason to question the candidates' ability to discern clearly their interests and gain advantage by tinkering with debate arrangements. Clinton's campaign strategists looked forward to the vice presidential debate in part because they felt, as did many other observers, that the more freestyle format would expose Vice President Quayle's weaknesses. But most reviewers felt Quayle performed well that evening.[11] The Bush campaign accepted the town meeting because it believed the president would do well in this setting. But Clinton dominated this debate, demonstrating a better grasp of the style and dynamics of this format. The Bush campaign also preferred the panel format to a single moderator. But after the final debate, the first half of which featured a single moderator with follow-up questioning and allowed direct exchanges between the candidates, Frederic Malek, a Bush campaign official, admitted that this format "gave the President more of a chance to stay on the issues than the other formulas."[12]

Although the candidates consider debates to be crucial for presenting their positions to the public and demonstrating their capacities to serve as president, they are also well aware that these forums can quickly undermine a candidacy. Accordingly, they usually take a defensive posture with respect to debate arrangements. "Winning the debates may be important to the candidates," says debate specialist Lee Mitchell, "but not losing is even more important."[13]

While the candidates want to make sure that they "can get their message out," they also want to avoid surprises and some even want to avoid free-ranging discussion and interaction (that is, unless a candidate believes that openness serves his or her interests, which is often the case with a challenger who trails in the race and is hoping to score a knockout in the debates; incumbents and front-runners, on the other hand, are rarely willing to provide such an opportunity). The candidates have therefore traditionally demanded restrictions (limiting the length of the questions, restricting the time of responses and rebuttals, prohibiting follow-up questions, and forbidding cross-questioning by candidates) in order to minimize intensive scrutiny or the possibility of a mistake.

How effective these restrictions are in serving the purposes candidates intend is difficult to assess. It is clear, however, that they diminish the amount of information conveyed to the public. " The debates in 1988 reflected the problems inherent in the current ad hoc system," writes Susan Spotts in a recent analysis of debates. "Since the candidates had the power to decide whether or not they would debate, they were able to dictate the terms of the debate. As a result, much of the informational value of the debates was lost."[14] And although the 1992 debates did a better job of educating voters, the conditions agreed to by the candidates retained many of the provisos of previous election campaigns, thus limiting the level of interaction among the candidates and hindering the ability of the moderators and panelists to move the candidates beyond their standard responses and to explore the implications of their answers.

More important, the ongoing practice of candidate negotiations every four years raises the possibility that the debates' quality will suffer as a result. "This continual negotiation [of debates]," says debate specialist Joel Swerdlow, "brings with it the danger that the public interest may get lost in the shuffle and that a particular candidate may be able to negotiate an unfair advantage."[15] This outcome is most likely when a challenger who trails in the polls is seeking to debate an incumbent president or an opponent with a large lead. In this scenario, the front-runner may be in so strong a bargaining position that his or her campaign representatives can essentially dictate terms and demand arrangements more favorable to their side. That would provide the disadvantaged candidate or public commentators with an opportunity to criticize the debates, which could diminish their luster in the public eye.

Even if neither contender gains an undue advantage, public regard for the debates can be affected by candidate agreements. Because candidates prefer to "play it safe," they tend to seek arrangements that minimize conflict or interaction and emphasize short statements or responses. This may cause the public to perceive the debates as little more than staged appearances that do more to promote the candidates' own agendas than the needs of the viewers. The perception is already held by many journalists and other debate analysts,[16] as well as some members of the public. For example, focus groups conducted during the 1992 campaign revealed that many voters believe that the debates should be arranged with the audience's interests in mind; that is, they believe that the public, not the candidates, should "own the debates" and that these should be geared to forcing the candidates to address questions the voters want to hear answered.[17] The same research also found "pronounced displeasure" with the traditional panel format and the time constraints imposed on candidate answers.[18] Should the vast majority of the public come to share these opinions, it might lose faith in these forums and the debates would lose their prominence. Instead of relying on the debates to the extent they do now to learn about the candidates, voters might choose other sources of information, heightening the role of paid television advertisements or other candidate-generated information. Negative public perceptions could eventually serve to improve the debate process by forcing candidates to adapt their strategies to meet the preferences expressed by voters, but this result might come at too high a cost in the form of delegitimization of the debates.

Critics of the current system are correct in arguing that the public interest would best be served if the planning of debates were left to an independent sponsor. This approach would ensure that debates were a part of every general election campaign, facilitating their early planning and allowing them to be scheduled at times necessary to attract the largest possible audience. It would also provide a better guarantee of equitable formats that would maximize informational content and ensure a level playing field for the candidates. In addition, it would eliminate the predebate debate among the candidates, or at least reduce this aspect of presidential campaigns to the bedrock decision of whether or not to participate.

However, the decision to debate, and under what conditions and formats, is considered by presidential candidates to be one of the most important tactical decisions in the general election campaign. Contenders are therefore reluctant to forsake their role in the decisionmaking process. Campaign strategists have attempted to support this position by arguing that direct involvement is the best way to ensure the collective interest of the candidates and the public in arrangements that are fair to all, as well as guarantee that the debates will reflect the dynamics of a particular election.[19] But the fact of the matter is that candidates know they have the opportunity to exert influence and are determined to do so. As Lane Venardos, vice president for hard news and special events at CBS, has observed, "the candidates have all the high cards, including the ultimate high card—whether to participate,"[20] and they are eager to play them in the pursuit of their individual political interests.

These political realities must be acknowledged in assessing the role of the Commission as the debate sponsor. While optimally the Commission would plan the debates without candidate interference, this conception fails to give due recognition to the political and strategic concerns that form the broader context of debate decisionmaking. While there is little argument against the view that candidates should adhere to voters' interest and accept any appropriate recommendation made by the Commission, it must be acknowledged that the debates are part of a political process. The public good, unfortunately, is not the sole determinant of campaign staging.

To recognize the partisan context within which any debate sponsor must operate is not to argue that the Commission on Presidential Debates is ineffective or plays an insignificant role in the process. The political environment neither obviates the need for an independent sponsor nor diminishes the value of such an organization in protecting the public interest in debates. In fact, the 1992 election demonstrates the Commission's worth and influence.

Indeed, the lesson of the 1992 experience is that the Commission's performance must be judged on the basis of a reasonable standard and expectations. The fundamental role of a debate sponsor is to represent the public interest in the process. Its major objective should therefore be to facilitate planning. The public interest is not served by the absence of debates, or by debate arrangements that cheapen the quality of debate or are designed to minimize the information made available to the voters. The sponsor's first and foremost concern should be to ensure that these forums are held at all during the general election campaign. To accomplish this end, it must educate the public about the need for debates and work to convince the candidates of the importance of participating. A sponsor should then work to develop alternatives and arrangements that promote the sorts of interaction among the candidates that would be most useful to voters in helping them gauge the views of each on the issues and the outstanding differences between the nominees. It should undertake the preparatory work necessary for producing the debates, including site selection, the identification of possible dates and time slots, and other logistical details. Finally, the sponsor should serve as an honest broker capable of resolving disputes between the candidates as well as being the advocate of the public interest.

The Commission fulfilled all of these responsibilities in the 1992 election. The organization went to great lengths to produce a proposal well before the national nominating conventions that, in its view, would best serve the public interest and provide a level playing field for the eventual party representatives. Its proposal, which called for a series of debates with a single moderator instead of a press panel format, incorporated the findings of Commission-sponsored research as well as other studies on formats that promote interaction between the candidates and thereby best convey information to the voters. It also worked to assist all parties involved in identifying potential sites as well as dates that would ensure a large audience by avoiding scheduling conflicts with the networks. By issuing the proposal early in the election cycle, the Commission sought to convince those involved in the debates, as well as the broader electorate, of the worthiness of its proposal, especially regarding the need for more debates than in previous elections and the need to move away from the press panel format.

The Commission undoubtedly hoped for the best-case scenario: that its suggestions would be accepted by the presidential nominees and that the campaign could proceed without the debates becoming a major issue. But it recognized that the candidates would probably want to discuss any proposals between themselves before agreeing to a final plan. By offering a plan that could at least serve as a starting point for developing the 1992 forums, it sought (with some success) to set the agenda for any debate discussions that would take place and thereby help facilitate the debate process.[21]

Soon after receiving his party's nomination, Bill Clinton accepted the Commission's plan, agreeing to all its provisions. This action helped legitimize the organization's role, as did the Clinton campaign's subsequent evocations of the plan and calls for the Commission to be a participant in any negotiations. The Commission proposal provided Clinton with a concrete, nonpartisan plan that could be used as leverage in pushing for debates, as well as marking a starting point for debate negotiations. According to Harold Ickes, the Commission "helped initiate the negotiations in early June when it issued its call for the debates. Obviously there was some delay on getting the negotiations under way but that is part of the political process. . . ."[22] Bobby Burchfield, the Bush campaign's counsel, also attested to the influence of the Commission's actions. "We were somewhat surprised," he admitted, "that the Commission's proposal, once it was floated, gathered its own momentum, [and] took on an appearance in the public eye and in the eye of the media as a mandate that the candidates either had to accept or reject."[23]

Throughout the early fall, the Commission maintained its efforts to facilitate an agreement between the candidates by continuing to call publicly for one, offering to serve as a broker between the parties, and drafting alternative proposals after the initial proposed dates were cancelled. Although the Bush campaign blocked the direct participation of Commission members in the negotiations, the plan eventually adopted tacitly recognized the influence of the original proposal by calling for a series of debates and experimenting with a single moderator. The candidates' agreement did retain some use of the panel format, which the Commission had rejected, but it also improved on the Commission's ideas by providing for the town-meeting debate.

Perhaps most important, the candidates in the end agreed that the Commission should serve as debate sponsor. While many groups and media organizations were willing to perform this function, it appears that, unlike in 1984 and 1988, there was little controversy on the issue of sponsorship; the Commission was the only potential sponsor seriously considered by the candidates. In fact, throughout the 1992 cycle the only alternative to merit serious attention was contained in the offer advanced by the television networks in the fall of 1991. This proposal, however, was less a challenge to the Commission's authority than a sincere effort by the networks to improve the process by coming to a joint agreement early to avoid major scheduling conflicts and other problems.

Had the Commission entered into an agreement with the networks, it might have compromised its position as an independent, nonpartisan agency and thus undermined its legitimacy and authority for the future. Yet, to some extent, the failure of the two groups to come to an agreement represented a missed opportunity for promoting the public interest in the debate process. Had the Commission and networks agreed on a proposal to be implemented under the auspices of the Commission, in all likelihood it would have called for a single moderator and no live audience, which would have significantly enhanced the educative potential of these forums. Furthermore, such a joint agreement might have strengthened the Commission's hand in dealing with the major-party candidates, since the organization would have been representing a plan that enjoyed the support of not only the networks but also the League of Women Voters, the group that had sponsored the debates prior to 1988, which came out in support of the original network initiative. Thus, all former sponsors of debates would have been united behind one plan, and although there was no guarantee that the candidates would have accepted it, particularly given the Bush campaign's adamance in asserting its demand for campaign-to-campaign negotiations, such an agreement could have made it more difficult politically for a candidate to hold out.

The Commission expressed a legitimate concern in deciding to reject the network's proposal on the basis of the potential conflicts inherent in network sponsorship. Indeed, the plan served to reinforce the need for an independent, nonpartisan sponsor like the Commission on Presidential Debates. Although the networks, or other media outlets for that matter, are fully capable of producing debates, their sponsorship raises troubling issues alluded to in earlier chapters, primarily the violation of the line between participation in and coverage of the process. This problem was summed up by Newton Minow and Clifford Sloan in their 1987 study of presidential debates.

> The networks have no more of a role to play in planning presidential debates than they do in planning nominating conventions. To be sure, networks have sponsored debates in the presidential primaries, and local media frequently sponsor local debates. The networks also regularly interview candidates on shows such as "Meet the Press," [or] "Nightline." . . . Nevertheless, in the general election, the central role of the media should be to *cover* the campaign— and the debates, as a critically important part of the

campaign. When the networks participate, as they did in 1960, in planning and sponsoring the debates, that role is blurred.[24]

The potential conflicts that might arise under network sponsorship have also been cited by Joel Swerdlow in his analysis of debate sponsors. He writes:

> The public . . . has a vital interest in knowing how debate negotiations are progressing. How would the network news departments discharge this responsibility when their own executives were conducting the negotiations? Would network correspondents feel free to criticize their bosses? Would they even want to? And after the debate, would network commentators openly analyze whether the network-devised debate format had actually served the public interest?[25]

Even if professional journalists could avoid these problems, questions still remain about the ability of the networks to serve the public interest. The networks place high priority on the revenue implications of scheduling and conceivably could prove unwilling to broadcast debates in time slots reserved for major sporting events or popular programs. For example, the 1992 network plan included no debates on a Sunday, when major sporting events are being broadcast and the viewership of regular programming is particularly high. In practice, CBS did not carry the first presidential debate because of a conflict with a major league baseball playoff game that went into extra innings, and NBC joined the debate late due to its football coverage.[26] The networks may also, as suggested by their 1992 proposal, use the debates to showcase their news anchors and correspondents to the exclusion of other moderators or print journalists. Or they might individually make other decisions that could adversely affect the debates, as when ABC decided in 1980 not to provide a live broadcast of the debate between Ronald Reagan and John Anderson.[27]

The major-party organizations have also been suggested as debate sponsors.[28] The rationale behind this proposal is that the party committees would have the best chance at institutionalizing the debates because of the symbiotic relationship they enjoy with their respective nominees. Although they do not have enough influence over their candidates to guarantee debates absolutely, they offer the best possibility of ensuring that the contenders will meet in debates every four years because of their central role in the presidential selection process. Advocates argue that presidential aspirants would be more likely to debate under party sponsorship because the candidates are closely tied to the party both in practice and in the public mind, so that a commitment made by the party to have its standard-bearer debate would place a greater obligation on the candidate than otherwise. The party organizations could even make debate participation a condition of nomination under party rules.[29] A further benefit of this approach is that it would provide the party organizations with a meaningful role in an election system that has become primarily candidate-centered.

The problem with this suggestion is that it places too much faith in the ability of the national party committees to influence the actions of their presidential nominees, and in the willingness of the party organizations to tie their candidates to a particular strategy. "As a matter of practice, philosophy, and practicality," says Swerdlow, "parties are extremely unlikely to impose their will on presidential candidates. . . . No rational party would urge its nominee to engage in a debate that decreased his chances of winning."[30] Even if the party did attempt to impose its will, for instance by adopting party rules that require the nominee to debate, this would have little effect on the candidates. Presidential nominees would feel free to ignore the party dictates, as they do now in deciding what portions of the platform to support. Or they would simply demand a change in the rules, a request with which the party would likely comply. Party sponsorship might also make it more difficult for independent or third-party candidates to participate in the debates, even when these aspirants were supported by a meaningful share of the electorate. At the very least, it might generate widespread perceptions that the debates are stacked in the favor of the two major-party nominees, which would undermine the legitimacy of the debates, or it could lead to major disagreements about inviting a third candidate, as it did in 1980.

As far as the question of sponsorship is concerned, the 1992 experience once again demonstrated that the public interest is best served by an independent, nonpartisan debate sponsor such as the Commission on Presidential Debates. An organization of this sort offers the best prospect of guaranteeing debates every four years by serving as an institutional advocate with a vested interest in seeing that these forums serve the needs of the electorate. By sponsoring debate-related research and presenting various alternative formats for consideration, the Commission encourages dialogue and thus improves public understanding of the role of debates in national elections. Such an understanding can fuel popular expectations with respect to debates, thereby increasing the pressure on candidates to agree to debate. The Commission also plays a role in helping to facilitate the debate process by issuing proposals that can serve as a starting point for candidate talks, as in 1992.

In fact, the events of 1992 served to enhance the Commission's legitimacy and stature, and underlined the need for such a sponsor. The Commission should prove to be even more effective in 1996. Because President Clinton publicly accepted the Commission's plan in 1992 and acknowledged its authority, it will be politically difficult for him to adopt a different position in 1996. Should he once again endorse it, it is likely that the Commission's plan will serve as the cornerstone for debate planning, rather than a mere point of departure, which would constitute another major improvement in the debate process and a valuable precedent for the future.

CHAPTER FIVE

PRESS COVERAGE OF THE DEBATES: OLD ISSUES, NEW TECHNOLOGIES

Presidential aspirants tend to view debates as a double-edged sword. On the one hand, they are without doubt the most widely covered events in a general election campaign. They attract an enormous amount of press attention both before and after they take place, which offers candidates an unparalleled chance to share their views with the electorate. Presidential nominees therefore look forward to the debates as their primary opportunities to address a truly nationwide audience.

Yet candidates also approach these forums with great caution, adopting what might best be described as a defensive attitude. Previous elections have demonstrated that occasions like these are filled with peril as well as opportunity. Candidates have learned that a misstatement or a few well-placed one-liners can overshadow all other aspects of a night's performance. This is largely because of the way the press covers the debates.

Reporters generally adopt a strategic perspective in covering debates. Before a debate, they concentrate on what each candidate hopes to accomplish in the session or what each "must do" given the contender's position in the race. Afterward, they tend to focus on how well the candidates fulfilled their objectives and to judge who won and who lost. Because they lack the column space or airtime to review the entire debate, most reporters attempt to summarize each by identifying what they consider to be the critical moments. Such moments may include direct confrontations between the candidates on a key issue or a response that outlines a major policy stance. But most often these take the form of well-timed one-liners, such as Ronald Reagan's "There you go again" quip in 1980 or Lloyd Bentsen's declaration in 1988 that Dan Quayle was "no Jack Kennedy." Or, even worse, a candidate may make a major gaffe, such as President Ford's statement about Soviet influence in Eastern Europe, or find themselves, like James Stockdale in 1992, "out of ammunition" on a particular question.

In an effort to provide their readers or audience with objective information, reporters often rely on the views of third-party analysts, including outside experts, representatives of each of the parties, and even other reporters or news commentators, to determine the most important moments in the debate, as well as winners and losers. They also rely on the results of public opinion surveys taken immediately after the debates, which in this era of high technology are often finished within hours so that the findings can be included in the first wave of news stories. The collective decision of the press as to how well a candidate did in a debate is thus not based on substance of argument, or on an analysis of how well the candidates articulated their positions and defined their differences. Instead it is usually based on a determination as to which candidate had the best sound bite, or dominated the defining moments, or exceeded predebate expectations, or did what he or she "had to do."

Consequently, beginning with the first presidential debate in 1960, when some reporters demonstrated more interest in Nixon's appearance and a makeup product called "Lazy Shave" than in the essence of the candidates' statements, political analysts have criticized the way the press reports on the debates. Media coverage has been attacked on a number of grounds, including charges that it tends to focus on style over substance, that too much coverage is given to the debate process and the candidates' debate over the debates, and that it tends to overemphasize the "horse race aspects," concentrating on who gained tactical advantage instead of discussing the policy issues raised by these forums. Although a complete discussion of debate coverage is beyond the scope of this paper, the criticism regarding "horse race" coverage warrants special consideration, especially in light of the 1992 experience and the rapidly expanding use of new technologies in the reporting of debates.

In recent elections, analysts have consistently charged that the press places too much emphasis on the strategic dimensions of the debates. According to Kathleen Hall Jamieson, one of the leading critics, the media's single-minded perspective consequently "reduce[s] debate coverage to three questions: who won? why? and what impact will the debate 'performance' have on the outcome of the election?"[1] She and other scholars contend that this approach minimizes the potential educational value of the debates in its emphasis on political tactics and concerns at the expense of real policy discussions. As Jamieson has stated, "this constricted focus on unanswerable and silly questions reduces the panorama of information gathered by all segments of the viewing public to irrelevant data."[2]

Scholars have condemned media coverage not only for its trivializing of substance, but also because "horse race" coverage tends to color viewers' perceptions of the candidates, as demonstrated by research on previous elections. The most well-known example is President Ford's blunder concerning Eastern Europe during the second presidential debate in the 1976 election. Studies have shown that the postdebate focus on this inappropriate statement had a major effect on voter opinion in the days following the debate.

The coverage of Ford's gaffe is not the only example of debate reporting that has elicited criticism. In 1980, ABC News conducted a "poll" after the Carter-Reagan debate in an attempt to determine which candidate had won. The findings, which were broadcast that same night on the network's late-night program *Nightline*, were the result of self-selected phone calls made by members of the public. The network established two 900-number telephone lines for viewers to ring up at a charge of fifty cents per call. One number counted those who thought Carter had won, the other those who thought Reagan had performed better. ABC's presentation noted that the poll was not scientific, but it did not describe the many flaws and inherent biases of its approach. For example, there was no effort made to sample a random cross section of voters; an individual could call more than once; some calls were recorded for the wrong candidate; the cost of the call might have discouraged poorer citizens from participating; and at the time the poll was conducted the hour was already late on the East Coast, which might have reduced the number of calls made from that region of the country. When the calls were tabulated the results showed that Reagan had won by a substantial margin. Whether these results were accurate is impossible to determine. Whether they had a

major effect on public perceptions is a matter of great controversy.[3]
But it is safe to say that they did little to help viewers comprehend
the substantive issues raised in the debate or the candidates' respective positions on topics of public concern.

Throughout the elections of the 1980s, media reports also devoted substantial time to the opinions and analyses offered by "spin doctors," representatives of the respective campaigns whose task is to
convince reporters that their candidate performed best in the debate.
In most instances, campaigns transport these individuals to the debate
site or recruit the assistance of well-known elected officials who plan
to attend, so that they can be available to reporters for interviews
before and after the function. Their role is to try to sell a party line,
a set of statements or "talking points" developed by campaign staffers
often before a debate even begins, and thus shape the tone and direc-
tion of the news coverage. In doing so, their primary goal is to convince reporters that their side won and to reinforce some of the points
made by their candidate in the debate, especially the most telling
charges or attacks against their opponents.

As a result, follow-up news coverage, especially in the 1984 and
1988 election cycles, presented voters with a barrage of opinions and
viewpoints as to who won and why, as well as competing analyses of
how the debate would affect each candidate's standing in the race.
Such treatment does little to clarify the issues raised in the debates
and offers no guidance to voters attempting to sort out the most
important aspects of the candidates' discussion. Rather, it encourages voters to focus on tactics and promotes the perception that these
events are but one aspect of a political game.

Early analyses of the 1992 coverage suggest that debate reporting
has improved. In this campaign, the press generally portrayed the
debates as important to voters, which was not always the case previously.[4] This change "is a good sign," says James Bernstein of the
Indiana University School of Journalism. "One of the main reasons for
having televised presidential debates is because of their value to voters. The more the news media recognize voters . . . as participants in
the debates, the greater legitimacy the debates will have."[5] Another
improvement cited by a number of observers was the move away from
a reliance on campaign spin doctors as sources of analysis on the candidates' respective performances and the meaning of the debates.
Instead of reporting the angle presented by campaign spokespersons
armed with predetermined talking points, many news organizations

turned to academic analysts, undecided voters, or others to examine what had occurred. A *Los Angeles Times* article even went so far as to declare that "spin is dead,"[6] an opinion affirmed by *Newsweek* media critic Jonathan Alter, who stated that such efforts to shape coverage had become "pointless and irrelevant to the process."[7]

The 1992 coverage, however, offered little evidence to suggest that the press was moving away from its emphasis on the strategic aspects of the debates. After the 1988 election, debate coverage was castigated for presenting voters with strategic information that may have unduly influenced their perceptions of the debates. For example, a number of networks displayed an electoral map projecting a major Republican victory as part of their coverage on the eve of the last presidential debate in 1988, which essentially told viewers either that the debate was inconsequential or that Dukakis would have to have an exceptional evening if he were going to improve his position in the race. Despite this criticism, electoral maps depicting projected outcomes were once again included in the predebate coverage of the final debate in 1992. According to Jamieson, these graphics "made it more difficult for voters to take the candidacies of [Bush and Perot] seriously in that evening's debate."[8]

CNN's 1992 debate broadcasts included an even more questionable practice. The cable network led into each of the presidential debates with a report from its polling analyst on the results of a daily tracking poll. This information was aired just as the candidates were walking onto the stage so that it almost appeared as part of the debate. It thus gave viewers a frame for structuring what they were about to see. In essence, the network told voters that President Bush was trailing in the polls and that Ross Perot was well behind the major-party candidates, information that was unnecessary for understanding the debates, which certainly might have colored voters' perceptions and gave cause to question whether the candidates would be fairly judged by those watching.

Newspaper accounts were not much better. A study by the Freedom Forum Media Studies Center of six leading newspapers, four major networks, and PBS concluded that "while the media covered the debates in detail, there was too much emphasis on the horse-race aspect of the events and not enough interpretation of events."[9] The study noted, for example, that "perhaps the common thread" running through newspaper accounts of the first presidential debate was "an apparent eagerness to emphasize Bush's 'behind-the-eight-ball' status."[10] A similar conclusion was reached by another study of five leading newspapers conducted at Emerson College. This analysis found that "conventional wisdom about Bush campaign failures and his 'horserace' position colored debate assessments," with Bush often described as "trailing," "confused," "defensive," and "desperate."[11] Bill Clinton, on the other hand, "although not always seen as impressive," was characterized as "comfortable," "confident," and "in command." Moreover, his performances in the debates "were seen to reflect a well-functioning campaign which could, in turn, predict professionalism and success in governing."[12]

The won-lost mentality was also evident from the heavy reliance placed on polling information. While many media outlets resisted the sound bites of spin doctors, they often replaced this form of analysis with information provided by their own focus groups. A number of news organizations sponsored sessions with members of the public, especially undecided voters, to solicit their views of the debates. The *Atlanta Constitution*, *Washington Post*, and *Miami Herald*, as well as other newspapers, brought small groups of undecided voters together to view the debates and share their opinions on the candidates' respective performances.[13] PBS's *MacNeil/Lehrer News Hour* featured, as a part of its regular coverage of each debate, an interview session with ten undecided voters who shared their thoughts on the previous night's forum. After the second presidential debate, CBS, in its evening news broadcast's "Eye on the Campaign" segment, showed excerpts of anchorman Dan Rather's meeting with a few voters yet to make up their minds in an empty Wrigley Field in Chicago, where he asked their opinions about the debate. NBC followed suit after the third presidential forum, broadcasting Tom Brokaw's discussion with three uncommitted voters on its evening news telecast.[14]

From the public's perspective, the best service a network can provide is to broadcast the debate and simply allow the voters to see the candidates and make their own judgments as to what they saw. But the networks have increasingly placed an emphasis on telling viewers how to judge the debate, presenting them with analysis as to what was most important and explaining why a candidate won or lost. Coverage of this sort can have a powerful influence on voter attitudes. It encourages voters to focus on certain aspects of the debates—or particular answers—at the expense of others and of broader assessments of the candidates. It can also alter voters' perceptions by presenting them with judgments that invite them to substitute collective opinion for their own independent thoughts.

Given these potential consequences of news coverage, an even more worrisome change in 1992 was the expanded use of instant polling techniques. A number of news organizations and networks used sophisticated, computerized "instant-response" technologies to gain more authoritative and scientific information as to what voters were thinking and who won each of the debates. These instant polling techniques have been used for some time by marketing research organizations and political campaign professionals to gauge public opinion, test new ideas or advertisements, or judge the effectiveness of a candidate's appearance in a debate or televised interview. However, they had not been a prominent component of the media reporting on debates until CNN added this dimension to its 1992 coverage in conjunction with the first presidential debate.[15]

During the first and third presidential debates, CNN monitored the pulse of a random sample of 480 registered voters, selected to reflect national opinion, through an instant, interactive polling technology, which was partly financed by a grant from the Markle Foundation. All of the participants in the survey were instructed to express their immediate feelings, their "likes" and "dislikes," about each answer given by a candidate throughout the debate. These opinions were registered via push-button telephone: respondents simply called a toll-free 800-number and, as they watched the debate, punched any number from one to nine on their telephone keypads, creating an opinion scale that ranged from a highly negative to a highly positive reaction for each answer. The responses were collected at a facility in Omaha and then almost immediately relayed to another company operating out of CNN's Atlanta newsroom, which interpreted the results and assisted in the development of linear graphic images, similar to a biofeedback chart with four separate lines, that could be superimposed on the videotape playback of the debate to show almost simultaneously a candidate's statement and the separate responses of both undecided voters and the Bush, Clinton, or Perot supporters.

Within minutes after the debate, CNN public opinion analyst William Schneider explained the poll to those watching the postdebate roundup and interpreted several graphs. These charts, which appeared side by side on the television screen with videotaped footage of a candidate speaking, presented voter reactions to particular statements. The graphs were thus used to select some of the big moments in the debate, as gauged by the respondents' immediate reactions, and to provide some insights into which statements the viewers liked or disliked.

CNN was not the only media outlet to use "continuous, on-line audience response" systems to monitor public reaction to the debates. The Norfolk *Virginian-Pilot* in cooperation with ABC News and Virginia Commonwealth University employed this technology during the second presidential debate, gauging the reactions of 104 selected undecided and weakly committed voters. The reactions of these citizens were summarized and plotted on a graph, which was superimposed on the recorded television image of the proceedings. Excerpts from the videotape were broadcast later that evening on ABC's *Nightline* to document public response to the event. Newspaper reporters constructed a running graphic of responses throughout the entire debate, annotated with excerpts of what was being said at the high and low points on the graph, and had it published on the front page the next morning.[16] As part of its "Rock the Vote" campaign, MTV used similar technology to report on the electronically recorded reactions of a group of Boston-area college students to the third presidential debate.[17]

A principal benefit of the new reliance on instant-response polling techniques is that it has provided journalists with an alternative to spin doctors and political pundits. As one study has suggested, it thus "reverses the traditional order [in coverage]: it places the citizenry, or at least some clearly defined portion of it, at the center of the ensuing discourse" generated by the debates. "Pundits are compelled, at a minimum, to take the audience response into consideration as they begin the process of interpreting the event."[18] These new techniques can avoid the major flaws and distortions that characterized earlier polling methods, such as the self-selected call-in used by ABC in 1980, if a representative sample is carefully chosen by those who conduct the survey.[19] They can also offer indications of the richness and texture of citizens' responses to various candidate statements, which help identify the issues of greatest importance to the electorate.

Yet instant-response technology is not without its limitations, and, like many other reportorial methods, it can be misleading when used improperly. It may, for example, exclude certain demographic groups or participants from particular regions, since respondents are required to have a push-button phone located near a television set. There is also some controversy as to how to interpret such polls. What is actually being measured? Survey instructions usually ask participants to react "positively or negatively to what you are hearing and seeing during the debate." Are respondents making their decisions strictly on the basis of what they saw or heard? Are they reacting to the content of a statement, rhetorical style, or a candidate's appearance?[20]

In addition, depending on how they are used and reported, these methods may produce distorted perceptions of the public's overall reactions. For example, a study of the results of the poll conducted at Virginia Commonwealth University found that Ross Perot's favorable score while speaking was generally the highest of the three presidential candidates. Perot tended to strike a resonant note with voters, who responded to his more folksy, tell-it-like-it-is approach. But a post-debate survey of the polling group showed that more individuals had decided to shift their support to Clinton than to Perot. The study thus argued that "voters may reach conclusions about a candidate that are very different from the 'sum' of their reactions to particular bits of information."[21]

Most important, the rise of instant-response technologies and other new methods of tapping into public opinion may exacerbate the tendency of the press to focus on who won or lost the debate. Armed with these new techniques, reporters may not be able to resist exploiting the information made available to them to declare even what specific statements might have been the key to victory for one candidate or another. It is likely that reporters would welcome the data developed through instant, interactive polling since this information is considered more objective than the opinions of campaign officials or in-studio commentators. Moreover, it would take much of the "guesswork" out of postdebate coverage; reporters would now have a standard—public response—for determining the critical statements in a debate or the defining moments.

New technologies may reinforce the recent trend toward viewing politics as an exercise in market research. They may also have an increasingly important influence on candidate behavior. Many observers of American politics already object that polls play too great a role in elections. Presidential campaigns, in particular, use polls not only to determine voter opinion on the nation's most pressing problems and various policy alternatives, but also to gauge the public response to various campaign messages, candidate statements, and political ads. If reporters and broadcasters make ever greater use of polling information to judge debate performances, candidates will undoubtedly respond in kind. This practice will therefore not only modulate the tone of debate coverage; it will also induce candidates to place even more emphasis on prepared sound bites and pretested lines in an effort to spark favorable audience reactions that will be reflected in postdebate coverage. A reliance on interactive polling will serve to reduce the level of spontaneity or the number of direct answers to posed questions in debates, which will further undermine the educational potential of these forums.

Finally, the use of instant polling undermines the role of debates in encouraging citizens to render independent judgments on the candidates and their proposals. Perhaps the most valuable feature of a debate is that it provides voters with an opportunity to see and hear the candidates. It thus constitutes an important vehicle for promoting self-guided voter decisionmaking. But this objective is severely threatened by the rise of the new technologies to assess collective voter opinion. Reporting this information immediately after the debate as part of a summary broadcast or in the next day's newspapers means that the electorate will be presented with conclusions as to what the majority thinks about the debates and the candidates' respective performances before most have even had time to digest the substance of the encounter, discuss it with others, and come to a decision in their own minds. Increasingly, individuals may defer to quickly formed collective judgments made on the basis of initial impressions. Such decisionmaking by proxy saps some of the vitality from an already fragile democratic process.

Unfortunately, unless the media begin to confront some of these issues and rethink their approaches to debate coverage, the prospects look disheartening. Given the rapid development of telecommunications and computer science, in the near future a television network will be able to broadcast the results of its interactive polling at essentially the same time as a debate. The technology now exists to superimpose instant-response polling graphs on "live" coverage with only a few seconds' delay. As television stations gain the capacity to show the debate and viewer response simultaneously, there may be a great incentive for some stations to try to "improve" debate coverage or provide viewers "with something more interesting or informative" by presenting graphs of voter responses alongside the actual debate. This intrusive addition would distract many viewers from the debate itself, especially in the initial period before the novelty wore off.

The possibilities and potential pitfalls of instantaneous polling have been described by Michael Delli Carpini of Columbia University and some of his colleagues.

> Imagine watching the candidates and how the public is reacting simultaneously on your television screen. Ostensibly, this is nothing more than providing voters with information about how their fellow citizens are responding to the debate. One might even argue that it could help transform the isolated act of watching television into a more communal experience, albeit an antiseptic one. On the other hand, it raises the very real specter of a forced consensus, of pressuring unsure or weakly committed citizens to go along with the crowd, of equating the *majority* opinion with the *correct* opinion.[22]

The potential flaw identified by Delli Carpini and others is inherent in many of the interactive techniques employed in recent debate coverage, including interviews with selected voters, focus groups, or more sophisticated instant-response approaches. Television journalists and newspaper reporters must therefore exercise caution in how they use such tools and report their findings, lest they further devalue the policy dimensions of the debates and their potential to educate the electorate.

To guard against this possibility, the press and media should give greater attention to the substance of the debates. Broadcasters should open their coverage by providing more information on the candidates' positions, a general summary of the campaign to date, and a discussion of the major issues in the race. This approach would give the audience a better and more informative context for viewing the debates, and would offer voters more than the current fare of pundits and reporters talking about what "we might expect to see" in the debate or what each candidate has to do to win.

The public would also be better served by fuller discussion after the debates. As Kathleen Hall Jamieson has suggested, postdebate "analyses should begin by summarizing the similiarities and differences between the candidates, and then indicate what was added to that knowledge by the clash of the debate."[23] Coverage should also expand on some of the most important issues raised in the debate, perhaps by broadcasting a discussion with policy experts or airing a report on the candidates' health care proposals or economic plans, so that the voters come away with a richer understanding of what is being offered for their consideration. Since it is probably inevitable that the networks will continue to sponsor their own polls and focus groups, the results of their findings might be included in a more well-rounded discussion of public attitudes. For example, the major networks might extend the debate broadcast to present a session conducted by a moderator with a polling group or audience where members of the public share their views and discuss what they witnessed. Such an approach might enliven the discourse associated with each debate and further encourage commentators to move away from horse-race-type analyses.

As with other suggested changes in the debate process, further efforts to promote coverage that enhances substance will help to ensure that debates fulfill their educational function and foster an informed electorate. To the extent that the debates achieve this purpose, they will continue to be viewed by the candidates, the press, and, most importantly, members of the public as pivotal events in the election process. If the public continues to regard them as valuable experiences, it will continue to demand debates, making it increasingly likely that they will be a permanent feature of the electoral process. Institutionalization, in turn, will provide the candidates, the Commission on Presidential Debates, the media, and other participants in the process with further opportunities to build on the success of the 1992 forums and provide the American electorate with even better debates in the future.

CHAPTER SIX

CANDIDATE PARTICIPATION

Under the current process for arranging debates there is no guarantee that debates will be held from one election cycle to the next. As a number of commentators have noted, every four years the presidential contenders will undoubtedly acknowledge the public's wishes by expressing their desire to debate and by offering assurances that debates will take place. But candidates will not agree to share a stage with each other until they are satisfied that it is in their political interest to do so. Consequently, each quadrennial election is characterized by a prolonged debate about the debates, which raises the possibility that they will not take place, either because one of the candidates refuses to appear, because the major-party nominees cannot agree on whether to invite some other challenger to participate, or because the candidates disagree on the details of the arrangements.

Thus, in each election the public faces the possibility that there will be no debates at all. This was the case from 1964 to 1972, when the candidate leading in the polls refused to debate his opponent. Or the candidates may decide to participate in only one or two debates late in the campaign, as occurred in 1980, when disagreement between President Carter and Ronald Reagan over independent John Anderson's participation in the forums led to only one debate between the major candidates in the waning days of the campaign.

Many debate specialists argue that debates are all but assured in the future as a result of public presumption, formed from the experience of the last five elections. These experts contend that debates have become such an accepted part of national elections that to do without them has become unthinkable. Harold Ickes, who worked with the Clinton campaign, has stated that "these [presidential] debates have been virtually institutionalized. I think they are almost mandatory now, and the pressure is enormous for candidates to participate."[1] Beverly Lindsey, who coordinated the debates for the Clinton-Gore campaign, expressed an even stronger view. "I think debates are institutionalized in that I don't think there's any way a candidate now can responsibly refuse to debate."[2] Bobby Burchfield of the Bush campaign agreed, declaring that "the candidates currently have the strongest possible incentive to debate, an incentive stronger than a regulatory or Commission on Presidential Debates mandate, and that is [that] debates are what the American public want. Any politician who cares to sail against that strong wind is going to pay a heavy price for it."[3]

Others, however, are not so sure. Tom Donilon, a member of the Dukakis negotiating team in 1988 and the Clinton group in 1992, has argued that, based on his experience, debates "are not at all inevitable in presidential campaigns." In his view, had the Bush negotiators' demands not been met in 1988, they "would have walked [out of the debate talks] easily, and probably wouldn't have paid a price."[4] Hal Bruno of ABC News, who moderated the 1992 vice presidential debate, has voiced the same concern. "While the 1992 debates resulted in a record number of viewers," he concluded, "I think we came close to not having any debates at all."[5]

While those views may be somewhat pessimistic, there is certainly no guarantee under the current system that candidates will decide that debates are in their best interest, or that they will agree to the number of encounters staged in the previous election. A candidate with a substantial lead in the polls may still decide that it is better strategically to incur the criticism for not debating, or to accept only one or two, than to agree to a series of debates that might provide an opponent with an opportunity to gain ground in the race. Conversely, a candidate trailing in the polls may decide that the best way to catch up is to rely on tactics other than debates, such as paid media and personal campaigning. Indeed, in 1992, the primary reason why Bush delayed in accepting Clinton's challenge was reportedly his campaign strategists' belief that the best way for the president to catch up was to spend on advertising and employ other tactics, and then, once the gap between the two had narrowed, agree to debate.[6]

These differences of opinion among informed students of the political process are the source of the controversy over whether anything further needs to be done to ensure future candidate participation. There is a wide consensus that the public interest is best served by guaranteeing debates in the future. The question is whether further action is needed or could be taken to preserve this interest. Most of the arguments in response revolve around the issues of whether candidate participation should be required by law and whether the procedures for including independent or minor-party candidates in these forums should be amended.

SHOULD PARTICIPATION BE MANDATED?

There is substantial disagreement as to the best means of fulfilling the objective of making debates a permanent feature of presidential campaigns. Many election watchers still share the conclusion advanced in reports issued by both the Twentieth Century Fund and the Commission on National Elections prior to the 1988 election that the best way to ensure that debates are made a fixture of the presidential selection process is to support a permanent independent sponsor like the Commission on Presidential Debates. Others, however, feel that the Commission has failed to fulfill its promise and that a more forceful remedy is needed. For example, James Karayn, who served as executive director of the 1976 debates for the League of Women Voters and was one of the earliest advocates of mandatory debates, initially upheld the view that an ongoing commission was the way to guarantee future debates. "It is essential," he wrote in 1979, "that there be a formal body invested with the clout to oblige candidates to debate."[7] But more recently he has expressed disappointment that the Commission lacks the power to compel candidates, and has concluded that "the Commission—unless it strengthens its power—cannot fulfill its own mandate."[8]

This concern over the Commission's lack of authhority has led some critics, like Keith Darren Eisner, to take a more vehement position, arguing that the time has come to adopt legislation to compel candidates to participate in debates.[9] The notion of a legislative mandate has received growing support in recent years. Democratic congressman Edward Markey of Massachusetts, a leading advocate of debate legislation, has said that "the public, which pays for the campaigns of presidential candidates, deserves and should demand substantive debates in return for its investment."[10] Similarly, the Markle Commission, in a report on the media and the electorate issued after the 1988 election, pointed out that "research shows the public pays more attention to the debates than any other campaign event." It therefore "recommend[ed] that public funding of campaigns be conditioned on candidate commitment to partici- pate [in debates] and that the debates become permanent future fix- tures of presidential campaigns."[11]

This notion, like many other proposals for improving debates, is not new. Senator Robert Dole of Kansas was apparently the first to introduce a proposal of this kind when he submitted S. 3127 to the 96th Congress during the general election campaign of 1980. This bill would have withheld public funds from presidential candidates who refused to debate under specified circumstances. At the time, Dole stated, "[T]hese funds were meant to allow the American people to be well informed on the issues and the candidates—not to finance a 'Rose Garden' strategy. . . . No debate, no dollars."[12] Dole presum- ably made this proposal in response to the refusal of President Carter to participate in a general election debate sponsored by the League of Women Voters that would have included John Anderson. Since it was designed to embarrass Carter, Congress never took it seriously.[13] After the election, Anderson expressed support for the idea of requiring presidential candidates to debate as a condition of receiving public funding.[14] Since that time, mandatory debate bills based on this premise have been regularly introduced in most Congresses.[15]

Two major debate bills were introduced in the 103d Congress. The first, H.R. 1753, titled the "Democracy in Presidential Debates Act of 1993," was introduced by Representative Timothy Penny, Democrat of Minnesota, and others on April 21, 1993. This bill would require presidential general election candidates eligible to receive public fund- ing to participate in two debates of at least ninety minutes each, with one to be held in September and another in October at least two weeks before the election. Vice presidential candidates would be required to participate in a single debate of at least ninety minutes, which would be held between the two presidential forums. The proposal also provides for participation by minor-party and independent candidates. These individuals would be included in the debates if they were on the ballot in at least forty states and were qualified to receive federal subsidy pay- ments from the Presidential Election Campaign Fund.

The other major bill, H.R. 2003, titled the "National Presidential Debates Act of 1993," was introduced by Representative Markey on

May 5, 1993. This proposal is simpler than Congressman Penny's plan, in that it stipulates only that candidates eligible to receive payments from the Presidential Election Campaign Fund must participate in three presidential and one vice presidential general election debates, which are to be sponsored by a nonpartisan organization. If a candidate fails to participate and is responsible "at least in part for such failure," that candidate and his or her running mate would be considered ineligible for further public funding payments and would have to reimburse the Department of the Treasury for the full amount of any payments previously made.

Because most constitutional scholars agree that mandatory debate legislation on its own would probably violate a candidate's freedom of speech (that is, a candidate's right not to speak or participate in a debate),[16] both of these proposals tie the mandate to the receipt of public subsidies. The need to create a linkage with public funding has encouraged some advocates of a mandate to pursue this alternative through campaign finance reform legislation. For example, Section 803 of S. 3, the campaign finance reform bill introduced in the 102d Congress, which was offered as an amendment to the original bill by Senator Bob Graham, Democrat of Florida, would have required candidates to participate in four presidential and one vice presidential debates as a condition of receiving public funding. This provision was included in the conference version of S. 3 that was passed by both houses in 1992 and subsequently vetoed by President Bush.[17] A similar provision was resurrected in the 103d Congress and was included in President Clinton's original campaign finance reform plan, which proposed that candidates who receive public funding be required to participate in three debates.[18] Section 703 of the "Congressional Campaign Spending Limit and Election Reform Act of 1993" would require the presidential and vice presidential candidates to agree in writing to participate in debates (three presidential and one vice presidential) in order to receive public funds for the general election campaign. As in Representative Markey's bill, this provision would be enforced by denying further payments and demanding repayment of any public funds in the event that the Federal Election Commission determines that either of the candidates of a political party was responsible "at least in part" for the failure to participate.[19]

Advocates of these proposals claim that a legislative mandate would substantially enhance the quality of national elections. Such a law, they contend, would eliminate any candidate posturing about whether to debate, since no candidate would be willing to forgo the tens of millions of dollars provided by the federal public financing program in exchange for not debating. The law would therefore guarantee debates as an integral part of the presidential selection process. This, in turn, would restore public confidence in political campaigns by creating the perception that the candidates are accountable to the electorate. Moreover, because debates are "a galvanizing force in the electoral process," the law would serve to heighten voter interest in an election and improve voter turnout.[20]

Supporters of mandates also generally argue that an obligation to debate is not an unreasonable burden, given the value of public financing in a presidential general election (which amounted to $55.2 million per candidate in 1992).[21] Citing the Supreme Court's 1976 ruling in *Buckley v. Valeo*, which upheld the limits on contributions and spending that accompany public funding, as well as other court decisions, they further assert that a debate requirement would easily pass constitutional muster as a legitimate condition of receiving public subsidies. They also contend that there is no violation of any First Amendment freedoms, since the proposal mandates only participation and places no restrictions on what views a candidate can express, including voicing a protest against forced debates.[22]

Additional evidence in support of federal legislation can be drawn from the recent experience in the New Jersey gubernatorial elections. In 1987, New Jersey adopted regulations that require candidates for governor who accept the substantial subsidies offered by the state's public financing program to participate in general election debates.[23] Under this provision, candidates must participate in two debates, each at least an hour long, between roughly the third week of September and third week of October, unless they agree that there is an emergency that interferes with the proposed scheduling period, in which case the second debate must be held no later than two days before the election. The statute charges the New Jersey Election Law Enforcement Commission with the responsibility of selecting a sponsor, which may include any organization (for example, the League of Women Voters, a news organization or broadcast outlet, or an association of news publications or television stations) that has not affiliated itself with a political party or endorsed a candidate for the office of governor. It also sets out sponsor selection procedures, a detailed timetable, and an enforcement procedure. The specific format of the debates, however, is left to the sponsor, who must inform the Commission and all candidates of the date, time, location, and rules for the debates. No plans can be made final without consulting representatives of the participating candidates, and final rules must be presented to the Commission and all candidates at least five days before each debate is to occur.

Since its adoption, the New Jersey plan has worked well. All of the eligible candidates have found the state's public subsidy to be sufficient inducement to agree to participate in the debates, which have been staged with a minimum of public argument and candidate posturing. In fact, in the 1993 race, Democrat Jim Florio, the incumbent governor, and his challenger, Republican Christine Todd Whitman, agreed to participate in three debates—one more than required by law—even though at the time Florio held a sizable lead in most statewide opinion polls. These debates, which were held during the period from October 7 to 24, were broadcast live to a statewide television audience and used a press panel format in the first two meetings and a less formal setting for the third, with the candidates seated at a table with two television news anchors who served as questioners.[24]

Despite the apparent success of the New Jersey law, some analysts question whether a federal statute would be as effective. The federal proposals submitted to date basically set forth general language requiring candidates to debate and stipulating the eligibility requirements for participation. They contain no details as to the procedures for selecting a sponsor, the means of determining the settings and formats of the debates, or the extent of candidate involvement to be allowed. As currently proposed, they would thus fail to achieve one major objective: eliminating the predebate debate among candidates.

A federal mandate would, however, do away with the most important sort of candidate posturing, the posturing over whether to debate in the first place. At the same time, it would no doubt provide the sponsor of the debates, as well as the candidates, with some leeway in determining the arrangements. The requirement to participate would therefore not hinder the adoption of innovative formats, nor would it lock in a particular structure that in some future election might have the effect of a favoring a particular candidate.

Some opponents of federal debate legislation object that such a law might lead to "micromanagement" of the debates by Congress. That is, Congress might use the opportunity afforded by a mandate to outline the process or procedures of the debates in greater detail. Scott Matheson of the University of Utah College of Law, for example,

has warned that the enforcement of any debate mandate might necessarily depend on further and more painstaking regulations.

> Although not dictating what a candidate must say, the debate
> ultimately may be required to take place on television, as a
> matter of law or simply as a practical matter. Moreover, there
> must be a definition of what constitutes a political debate.
> That is, must the candidates appear together, must the
> debates concentrate on prescribed topics such as economic
> policy or arms control, and must there be a moderator? Who
> decides these questions? If substantial discretion is left to the
> parties, the candidates, or the sponsor, what happens and
> who decides if the debates do not meet what the lawmakers
> had in mind in mandating debates? The point is that in addi-
> tion to decreeing that "There must be debates," the govern-
> ment may not be able to escape the task of deciding and
> enforcing format and topic questions.[25]

[margin note: what is a debate]

If Congress does decide to provide more specifics than suggested in
the proposal at hand, some of the flexibility of the current process
may be lost, and it may become difficult to adapt the structure of the
debates to reflect new research and changing technologies.[26] A more
detailed regulatory approach would also raise legitimate questions
as to whether Congress was interfering "in a fundamental way with the
candidates' free speech and political process."[27] Government-imposed
guidelines, especially if related to format, might be interpreted as a
kind of "time, place, and manner regulation" that affects free speech
and is thus constitutionally challengeable.[28] Matheson therefore con-
cludes that legislation that leaves "as much possible discretion over
these matters to the political parties, candidates, and private debate
sponsors would be the constitutionally safest course."[29]

Yet even if this course were adopted, a federal debate mandate
might not withstand constitutional scrutiny. Some legal analysts claim
that any linking of public subsidies to a requirement to debate essentially places an unconstitutional "involuntary condition" on candidates
because an office seeker does not have a realistic choice as to whether
to accept public funding in the context of presidential campaigns
these days.[30] Whatever the case, it is likely that any federal legislation
will end up in the courts before it is implemented.

[margin note: will end up in the courts.]

Regardless of the constitutional implications, many observers
argue that federal legislation is no longer needed to guarantee

debates and that such a statute would simply serve as another example of unnecessary regulation of the political process. Seeing the public pressure for debates, which is likely to intensify as a result of the 1992 experience, plenty of people feel that a federal mandate would be of little benefit at this time. There is in any case no guarantee that the provision obligating participation could be effectively enforced. For instance, Martin Plissner of CBS News has reflected that if the candidates cannot come to terms on the many negotiable conditions that would continue to characterize the debates, it may be difficult to determine which candidate is the obstructive one.[31] A failure to reach agreement might produce an enforcement action in the midst of a campaign, which would serve as a distraction that drew public attention away from more substantive issues. Many share Sander Vanocur's view that the best solution is the public accountability inherent in the current system. "If people don't want to debate, then let them take responsibility for that. But don't get legislation that penalizes them by barring funds for their use."[32]

Whether legislation that ties public funding to participation would lead to micromanagement of the debates and major problems of enforcement is in part a matter of speculation. These problems have certainly not appeared in New Jersey, where a more detailed regime than those being proposed for presidential candidates has been in effect for a number of years. Nor does it seem that requiring participation in a series of debates is an especially onerous burden to put on the candidates, in view of the benefits of public funding and the arguments of many informed participants that a de facto institutionalization of debates has already taken place.

Moreover, the concerns of skeptics must be weighed against the voters' right to ensure that candidates submit their views to public scrutiny. In this respect, a federal law requiring participation might reinforce the notion that candidates are ultimately accountable to the people whose votes they solicit and do have an obligation to provide opportunities to see them present and defend their views.

SHOULD NON-MAJOR-PARTY CANDIDATES BE INCLUDED?

No minor-party candidate has ever participated in a presidential general election debate with the major-party candidates. Although two independent candidates, John Anderson in 1980 and Ross Perot in 1992, have been invited to participate, none of the nominees of the minor parties that run candidates in each presidential election has shared a stage with one of the major-party contenders. Minor-party candidates have predictably been counted among the leading supporters of federal debate legislation as a means of gaining entry into the presidential debates process. The New Alliance Party, for example, supports the establishment of legislative provisions that set forth objective criteria for determining candidate participation and has endorsed the basic concepts of Representative Penny's bill, which would guarantee eligibility to participate to any candidate that qualified for the ballot in at least forty states, received federal funds, or raised at least $500,000 in private contributions.[33] Even the Libertarian Party, which opposes "the entire concept of federal funding of campaigns," has said that candidates who accept federal money should be required to debate and that their party's presidential candidate would attempt to qualify for federal matching funds if that would facilitate partaking in nationally broadcast debates.[34]

The call for federal legislation represents minor-party candidates' increasing frustration with the presidential debates process. For years, these candidates or their respective party representatives have asserted their right to participate in debates. But despite overt protests, a number of court challenges, and other efforts to raise public awareness of their position, there is apparently little public interest in seeing these candidates share a stage with the major-party nominees during the course of a general election. As a rule, the nominees of the major parties do not believe that debates should be used to introduce candidates and their platforms to the electorate. Sponsors have generally joined in this view, arguing, perhaps justifiably, that candidates must demonstrate adequate public support to merit inclusion in these important national forums.

Before 1992, the primary role of minor-party candidates in the presidential debates process was to serve as bargaining chips in the negotiations between the major contenders. This is one of the reasons why the decision to include Ross Perot in the 1992 debates was so surprising. Instead of opposing Perot's inclusion, both Bush and Clinton welcomed his participation and invited him and his vice presidential running mate, James Stockdale, to take part "in anticipation" of approval by the Commission on Presidential Debates. Neither major-party nominee apparently wanted to risk offending Perot's supporters. Their decision was independently affirmed by the Commission when its advisory panel determined that Perot met the criteria for candidate eligibility established before the 1992 general election.

The decision to invite Perot to debate was challenged by a number of minor-party candidates who alleged that the Commission had unfairly discriminated against them. They as well as other observers who supported the inclusion of minor-party challengers protested that the Commission, headed by former chairmen of the Democratic and Republican National Committees, displayed a bias toward the major parties and failed to represent the views of minor-party candidates. One critic stated that "the circumstances of Perot's inclusion smacked of manipulation by the two major-party candidates" and "certainly cast doubt" on the Commission's independence.[35] Those who opposed the Commission's decision also claimed that its eligibility criteria were too subjective and that more objective standards, such as the number of state ballots a candidate had made, or a mathematical possibility of winning (meaning that the presidential hopeful's name appears on enough state ballots to reach a total of at least 270 electoral votes), or some fund-raising measure, should have been used. Any of these approaches would have ensured additional minor-candidate participation. For instance, like Perot, Libertarian Andre Marrou had qualified for the ballot in all fifty states and the District of Columbia, and he had raised more money than Perot in contributions from supporters. Lenora Fulani of the New Alliance Party had also raised more money in private contributions than Perot, had earned close to $2 million in federal matching funds during the primaries, and had qualified for the ballot in at least forty states. These candidates contended that Perot was included in the debates simply because of his personal wealth, which allowed him to purchase large blocks of network television time.[36]

Thus, although most observers believe that the system handled the issue of Perot's participation in the debates relatively well, the 1992 experience did not silence the continuing debate over minor-candidate participation in these forums. And it is unlikely that this issue will be resolved to the satisfaction of all parties concerned in the forthcoming elections, since the controversy is largely framed by the tensions inherent in the theory and practice of democratic politics.

In theory, minor candidates should be included in the debates since they have a right to present their views to the electorate just as the major party candidates do. One purpose of debates, after all, is to help the voters make a decision by exposing them to the candidates in a common setting that allows direct comparison among those seeking the nation's highest office. By including all contenders, the debates the nation's highest office. By including all contenders, the debates would expand voters' choice and perhaps thereby enliven the debates as well. As legal analyst Susan Spotts has stated:

> Third-party candidates have the potential for improving the informational and educational quality of the debates in two ways. First, third-party candidates could raise issues often avoided by the major-party candidates and force discussion of the various candidates' positions on these issues. Second, allowing the participation of candidates outside the two major parties would expose the voters to a broader spectrum of views. From this broader spectrum, voters whose interests may often be ignored by the major parties will have the opportunity to discover a candidate who may better represent their concerns.[37]

The history of minor parties in America certainly demonstrates their value in expanding the dialogue and contributing to the public agenda. Advocates of third parties maintain that these benefits can only be achieved if the views of these parties are made known to the electorate. One of the best ways of fulfilling this objective is to include minor-party candidates in the debates.

While sympathetic to the arguments advanced in support of including nonmajor candidates in the debates, most debate experts note that it is impractical to include even a small proportion of those running for president in any election year. In 1988, for example, about 280 people filed statements with the Federal Election Commission indicating that they considered themselves to be presidential candidates. Of these individuals, 168 actually declared as candidates, and 23 appeared on the ballot in some state. As a practical matter, some criteria must be established to determine which candidates have extensive enough support to be considered "significant" and thus merit consideration for inclusion in the debates.

Furthermore, many analysts warn that expanded participation may actually undermine the educational value and quality of debates. In their view, a debate serves the public interest only if it provides voters with a meaningful choice and information that helps them in casting their ballots. A multicandidate debate, especially one including more than three or four candidates, may not prove to be particularly helpful. In such a debate, each candidate will have less time to explain his or her positions, fewer issues are likely to be covered, the viewer will probably be presented with a number of conflicting view-points, and the differences between the candidates may be more difficult to discern as a result. While some of these concerns might be offset by increasing the length of each debate, longer debates might lead to a decline in the number of viewers or the intensity with which they pay attention to the proceedings.[38]

Debate sponsors have tried to strike a balance between the claims of non-major-party candidates and the need to provide the electorate with a meaningful forum by developing some sort of criteria to determine which candidates enjoy enough public support to warrant an invitation to the debates. The problem is that "no magic formula exists."[39] Some minor-party candidates support a strict set of criteria, such as those contained in Representative Penny's debate bill. But whatever standards are set, they will simply encourage candidates to adapt their campaign strategies to try to conform to the guidelines and qualify for the debates.[40] They are therefore likely to produce a number of candidates who qualify but enjoy little public support and have no realistic chance of winning the election.

Advocates of minor parties argue that standards like those contained in Representative Penny's bill would have resulted in only two additional candidates qualifying for the 1988 and 1992 presidential debates, one representing the Libertarian Party and another representing the New Alliance Party.[41] But this may not be the case in the future as candidates reorient their strategies to clear these relatively simple hurdles. Minor-party candidates have been increasingly successful in recent years in their efforts to gain a position on state ballots or to qualify for public subsidies because of recent changes in ballot access laws and the relatively low fund-raising threshold (a total of $100,000 raised in $5,000 increments through small contributions from at least twenty states) needed to qualify for federal matching funds.[42] These standards should be even more attainable in the future, as states continue to revise their ballot access laws to make things easier for candidates and as the threshold for federal matching funds becomes ever less burdensome relative to the overall costs of a campaign.

The Commission on Presidential Debates has recognized the potential problems posed by strict indicators and has sought to address these concerns by developing a set of broad criteria for determining participation. These criteria assess the significance of a candidacy through varied measures designed to determine the extent of a candidate's national organization, signs of a candidate's national newsworthiness or viability, and level of public support (see Appendix). These standards seek to ensure that those who have a "realistic"—that is, a "more than theoretical"—chance of winning an election are included in the debates. In an effort to ensure the fair implementation of these guidelines, the Commission leaves the determination to an advisory panel of academic experts, journalists, and other participants in the political process, who must review candidates on the basis of each one.

Minor-party advocates charge that the Commission's standards create a catch-22 situation for third parties or independents. They observe that a candidate needs a significant level of press coverage or public support to qualify for debates, but in order to generate such coverage and support in the context of modern elections, a candidate needs the legitimacy and attention that comes from participating in the debates. Most analysts, however, disagree with the premise of this argument and insist that the purpose of a general election debate is not to launch a candidacy or otherwise showcase someone who lacks meaningful public support. Frank Fahrenkopf of the Commission on Presidential Debates has stated that "it is the view of the Commission that the purpose of the general election presidential debates is not to provide a springboard for a relatively unknown candidate. It is to give the American public information about those people likely to be elected president, and that is why we set up . . . the elaborate criteria, some standards, that had to be applied first by an independent group."[43] Says Diana Carlin of the University of Kansas, "In my view, the general election debates are the point at which voters are making their final decision, are confirming the decisions that they have already made and are feeling better about for whom they are going to vote. It is not necessarily a springboard . . . or a way of suddenly saying: 'Here is another option when you are two weeks out [from election day].' That should take place earlier."[44]

The public seems to share the view that the time for non-major-party candidates to build support is at the outset of the campaign season and not during the general election debates. Focus groups conducted after the 1992 election found that many participants believed that minor party candidates should have an opportunity to express their views earlier in the process, such as during the primaries, rather than when voters are making a final decision.[45] Debates are particularly valuable in helping voters make a choice in the presidential race because they focus the electorate's attention on the major contenders. The benefit should not be diminished by turning these forums into multicandidate sessions that include challengers with no more than a hypothetical chance of winning the race.

The Commission has thus established what seems to be a reasonable and pragmatic set of standards for determining whether a non-major-party candidate should be included in the debates. Essentially, candidates must demonstrate that they have a viable campaign and a better than theoretical chance of winning the election. Candidates who meet these thresholds will be invited to participate regardless of their party affiliation or lack thereof. These guidelines make a concerted effort to balance a due regard for minor-party candidates with the fundamental (educational) purpose of a presidential general election debate.

This is not to argue that minor-party candidates should be denied an opportunity to share their views and make themselves available to those voters who might be interested in learning more about them and their positions. But a presidential general election debate is not the appropriate occasion for introducing these candidates to the electorate. Instead, these candidates should be given some vehicle for exposing the broader public to their views earlier in the election year. As Kathleen Hall Jamieson has commented, "the problem now is the so-called third-party candidates don't have the opportunity to build a following in order to ultimately pass the threshold test for the general election."[46]

One way to meet these concerns is to encourage broadcast debates among the most prominent minor-party candidates, so that interested members of the public can have an opportunity to hear their views. This approach was first suggested by the 1964 report of the American Political Science Association's Commission on Presidential Debates and has been regularly reiterated by debate authorities since that time.[47] Joel Swerdlow, for one, wrote in a 1983 study of presidential debates sponsored by the Twentieth Century Fund that such a debate might be a means of facilitating minor-party candidates' access to network coverage.

> [S]ignificant third-party candidates could debate one another—or any major-party nominees who decided to attend—in a debate televised in the late evening, or during

the day on a Saturday or Sunday. The audience would be relatively small, and all three of the networks might not provide full coverage. But such a debate would certainly offer third-party candidates their largest audience of the campaign. It would also help them build for the future, so that after late-night appearances in two or three presidential elections, a third party might qualify for prime-time exposure. . . . If public opinion coalesces in support of a series of debates that offers access for minor-party nominees who are significant but not serious contenders, the networks might conclude that all of the debates are sufficiently "newsworthy" to warrant live broadcast.[48]

Since Swerdlow's study, minor-party candidates' prospects of gaining public exposure through debate have improved owing to an expansion of the number of networks and news organizations available to sponsor or carry such a forum. For instance, during the 1992 election, C-SPAN sponsored a debate among the non-major-party candidates who had a "numerical" chance of winning the electoral college. Andre Marrou of the Libertarian Party and Lenora Fulani of the New Alliance Party met that standard and were invited to participate. Their meeting was not broadcast by the major networks, but it was aired by CNN and C-SPAN.

The proliferation of broadcast outlets has yielded greater opportunities to gain exposure beyond debating. In 1992, Marrou, Fulani, and John Hagelin of the Natural Law Party each received some coverage on C-SPAN and CNN through broadcast interviews or feature reports that appeared on such programs as CNN's daily political journal, *Inside Politics*. Local cable access channels and the rapidly growing number of daily talk shows also constitute opportunities for publicity in future elections. The problem from the perspective of the candidates involved, however, is that many news outlets still fail to provide them with adequate coverage. The Marrou-Fulani debate received hardly any attention from the major news organizations. Leading newspapers—the *New York Times*, *Washington Post*, *Chicago Tribune*, and *Los Angeles Times*—did not even print a transcript of the debate.

In future elections, minor-party and independent candidates should be given greater media exposure than they have received in past election cycles. News organizations and other groups should consider sponsoring debates among the leading minor-party standard-bearers before the general election campaign. Such actions will help ensure that these candidates have an opportunity to share their views with the electorate and will thus give them a better opportunity than they have had to try to build support and gain a broad enough following to be included in nationally televised presidential debates.

CONCLUSION

The 1992 presidential election once again demonstrated that debates are a valuable means of providing information to voters. These forums spurred public interest in the presidential campaign, generated substantial public discussion about the relative merits of the candidates, and helped millions of Americans make up their minds as to which candidate to support. They offered the electorate information and insights into the candidates that it could not have received from any other event or source available since face-to-face confrontations often turn out to be most meaningful to voters. And, perhaps most important, in a time when presidential campaigns are increasingly conducted through television ads, photo opportunities, and other techniques that serve to distance the candidates from the electorate, debates helped to maintain the bonds between them, and even gave a group of voters a chance to question the contenders directly before a national audience of their fellow citizens. No other event in the presidential campaign created such a positive response among the electorate, or made the candidates so accountable to those they are elected to serve.

The 1992 debates are particularly noteworthy for the precedents they established. For the second election cycle in a row, the debates were sponsored by the Commission on Presidential Debates, enhancing the Commission's status and increasing the likelihood that it will continue to perform this role. The formats used in the debates constituted a major step in breaking away from the press panel formats that have characterized modern televised debates since their inception and

155

revealed that innovative approaches can benefit the candidates as well as the viewers. Moreover, the second presidential debate with its extraordinary town-meeting approach exploded the myth that voters are not capable of directly participating in the process and questioning candidates on their own. The 1992 experience thus paves the way for further public participation down the road, which may prove to be an important step in the broader mission of trying to restore public confidence in the electoral process.

Yet if debates are to achieve their potential as vehicles for informing the electorate and are to have an effect on the way the majority views the political system, the actions taken to improve them in 1992 must be continued and expanded in forthcoming elections. The Commission on Presidential Debates, the candidates, and other participants in the process must be encouraged to pursue efforts to explore new approaches, format innovations, and additional means of making these forums more meaningful and valuable to the public. The press and media must reexamine the ways they cover debates and adopt changes that emphasize the substance rather than the gamesmanship of elections. In addition, more imaginative ways of involving the citizenry need to be developed to ensure that candidates address the questions foremost in the public mind and provide voters with the information they are seeking.

The 1992 debates represent a significant improvement over those of the previous decade. By following their example, the 1996 debates can be even better.

COMMISSION ON PRESIDENTIAL DEBATES' CANDIDATE SELECTION CRITERIA FOR 1992 GENERAL ELECTION DEBATE PARTICIPATION

A. INTRODUCTION

The mission of the Commission on Presidential Debates ("the Commission") is to ensure, for the benefit of the American electorate, that general election debates are held every four years between the leading candidates for the offices of President and Vice President of the United States. The Commission sponsored three such debates in 1988 and has begun the planning, preparation, and organization of a series of nonpartisan debates among leading candidates for the Presidency and Vice Presidency in the 1992 general election.

The goal of the Commission's debates is to afford the members of the voting public an opportunity to sharpen their views of those candidates from among whom the next President or Vice President will be selected. The Commission has determined that this voter education goal is best achieved by limiting debate participation to the next President and his or her principal rival(s).

A Democratic or Republican nominee has been elected to the Presidency for more than a century. Such historical prominence and sustained voter interest warrants the extension of an invitation to the nominees of the two major parties to participate in the Commission's 1992 debates. Consistent with the voter education goals its debates are designed to serve, the Commission also will invite nonmajor party candidates, if any, who have a realistic chance of winning the general election to participate in one or more of its 1992 general election debates.

With the assistance of an advisory committee chaired by Harvard Professor Richard Neustadt, the Commission has developed nonpartisan criteria upon which it will base its decisions regarding selection of nonmajor party candidates to participate in its 1992 debates. These criteria contemplate no quantitative threshold that triggers automatic inclusion in a Commission-sponsored debate. The purpose of the criteria is to identify nonmajor party candidates who have demonstrated a realistic chance of being elected the next President and Vice President of the United States. The realistic chance need not be overwhelming, but it must be more than theoretical. The Commission will employ a multifaceted analysis of potential electoral success, including a review of (1) evidence of national organization, (2) signs of national newsworthiness and competitiveness, and (3) indicators of national enthusiasm or concern, to determine whether a candidate has a realistic chance of election.

Judgments regarding a candidate's election prospects will be made by the Commission on a case-by-case basis. However, the same multiple criteria will be applied to each nonmajor party candidate. Initial determinations with respect to candidate selection will be made after the major party conventions and approximately contemporaneously with the commencement of the general election campaign. The number of debates to which a qualifying nonmajor party candidate will be invited will be determined on a flexible basis as the general election campaign proceeds.

B. 1992 NONPARTISAN SELECTION CRITERIA

The Commission's nonpartisan criteria for selecting nonmajor party candidates to participate in its 1992 general election presidential debates include:

1. *Evidence of National Organization*

The Commission's first criterion considers evidence of national organization. This criterion encompasses objective considerations pertaining to the eligibility requirements of Article II, Section 1 of the Constitution and the operation of the electoral college. This criterion also encompasses more subjective indicators of a national campaign with a realistic prospect of electoral success. The factors to be considered include:

a. Satisfaction of the eligibility requirements of Article II, Section 1 of the Constitution of the United States.

b. Placement on the ballot in enough states to have a mathematical chance of obtaining an electoral college majority.

c. Organization in a majority of congressional districts in those states.

d. Declaration of a third party or independent candidacy before the major party conventions, party primaries or state conventions, and eligibility for matching funds from the Federal Election Commission.

e. Declaration of an independent candidacy after a major party convention by disaffiliating from the party and securing a share of national delegates, pledges of financial support, eligibility for federal funding, and endorsements by federal and state officeholders.

2. *Signs of National Newsworthiness and Competitiveness*

The Commission's second criterion endeavors to assess the national newsworthiness and competitiveness of a candidate's campaign. The factors to be considered focus both on the news coverage afforded the candidacy over time and the opinions of electoral experts, media and non-media, regarding the newsworthiness and competitiveness of a candidacy at the time the Commission makes its invitation decisions. The factors to be considered include:

a. The professional opinions of the Washington bureau chiefs of major newspapers, news magazines, and broadcast networks.

b. The opinions of a comparable group of professional campaign managers and pollsters not then employed by the two major party candidates.

c. The opinions of representative political scientists specializing in electoral politics at major universities and research centers.

d. Column inches on newspaper front pages and exposure on network telecasts in comparison with the major party candidates.

e. Published views of prominent political commentators.

3.   *Indicators of National Public Enthusiasm or Concern*

The Commission's third criterion considers objective evidence of national public enthusiasm or concern. The factors considered in connection with this criterion are intended to assess public support for a candidate, which bears directly on the candidate's prospects for electoral success. The factors to be considered include:

a. The findings of significant public opinion polls conducted by national polling and news organizations.

b. Reported attendance at meetings and rallies across the country (locations as well as numbers) in comparison with the two major party candidates.

Adopted: June 4, 1992

NOTES

CHAPTER ONE

1. For background on the early history of political debates, see Kathleen Hall Jamieson and David S. Birdsell, *Presidential Debates: The Challenge of Creating an Informed Electorate* (New York: Oxford University Press, 1988); Joel L. Swerdlow, "The Strange—and Sometimes Surprising—History of Presidential Debates in America," in Joel L. Swerdlow, ed., *Presidential Debates: 1988 and Beyond* (Washington, D.C.: Congressional Quarterly, 1987).

2. Jamieson and Birdsell, *Presidential Debates: The Challenge*, p. 90. Thomas H. Neale also states that this debate was carried by the ABC, NBC, and Mutual radio networks (*Campaign Debates in Presidential General Elections* [Washington, D.C.: Congressional Research Service, June 1993], p. 1), but Lee M. Mitchell includes a fourth network, CBS (*With the Nation Watching: Report of the Twentieth Century Fund Task Force on Televised Presidential Debates* [Lexington, Mass.: D. C. Heath and Company, 1979], p. 28).

3. Jamieson and Birdsell, *Presidential Debates: The Challenge*, p. 90.

4. *With the Nation Watching*, p. 28.

5. Susan A. Hellweg, Michael Pfau, and Steven R. Brydon, *Televised Presidential Debates: Advocacy in Contemporary America* (New York: Praeger, 1992), p. 2.

6. *With the Nation Watching*, p. 29.

7. Ibid., p. 30.

8. 47 U.S.C. 315(a).

9. See Charles M. Firestone, "Legal Issues Surrounding Televised Presidential Debates," in Swerdlow, *Presidential Debates: 1988 and Beyond*, p. 17.

10. The legislation, Senate Joint Resolution 207, was passed by the Senate on June 27, 1960, and adopted by the House on August 22. Two days later, President Eisenhower signed the bill, which became Public Law 86–677. See Neale, *Campaign Debates in Presidential General Elections*, pp. 1–2.

11. *With the Nation Watching*, pp. 30–31.

12. Newton N. Minow and Clifford M. Sloan, *For Great Debates: A New Plan for Future Presidential TV Debates* (New York: Priority Press, 1987), p. 10.

13. For a discussion of these details, see ibid., p. 13; Hellweg, Pfau, and Brydon, *Televised Presidential Debates: Advocacy*, p. 3; Sidney Kraus, *Televised Presidential Debates and Public Policy* (Hillsdale, N.J.: Lawrence Earlbaum Associates, 1988), p. 38.

14. CBS sponsored the first debate, NBC the second, and ABC the final two.

15. Minow and Sloan, *For Great Debates*, p. 10.

16. *With the Nation Watching*, p. 32.

17. Minow and Sloan, *For Great Debates*, p. 10.

18. Theodore H. White, *The Making of the President 1960* (New York: Atheneum, 1961), p. 289.

19. David J. Lanoue and Peter R. Schrott, *The Joint Press Conference: The History, Impact, and Prospects of American Presidential Debates* (Westport, Conn.: Greenwood Press, 1991), p. 12.

20. Quoted in ibid.

21. Elihu Katz and Jacob J. Feldman, "The Debates in the Light of Research: A Survey of Surveys," in Sidney Kraus, ed., *The Great Debates: Kennedy vs. Nixon, 1960* (Bloomington, Ind.: Indiana University Press, 1977), pp. 173–223.

22. Lanoue and Schrott, *Joint Press Conference*, p. 13. A recent study, however, has challenged this widely held conclusion. See David L. Vancil and Sue D. Pendell, "Winning Presidential Debates: An Analysis of Criteria Influencing Audience Response," *Central States Speech Journal* 38, no. 1 (1987): 16–27.

23. Minow and Sloan, *For Great Debates*, p. 11.

24. Kurt Lang and Gladys Engel Lang, "Reactions of Viewers," in Kraus, *Great Debates*, pp. 313–30.

25. Minow and Sloan, *For Great Debates*, p. 12.

26. Ibid.

27. *With the Nation Watching*, p. 34.

28. Federal Communications Commission, *Aspen Institute*, 55 F.C.C. 2d 697 (1975).

29. Firestone, "Legal Issues Surrounding Televised Presidential Debates," p. 20.

30. Ibid., p. 21.

31. See Hellweg, Pfau, and Brydon, *Televised Presidential Debates: Advocacy*, p. 5; Minow and Sloan, *For Great Debates*, p. 21.

32. Lanoue and Schrott, *Joint Press Conference*, p. 19.

33. Minow and Sloan, *For Great Debates*, p. 22.

34. *With the Nation Watching*, p. 96.

35. Hellweg, Pfau, and Brydon, *Televised Presidential Debates: Advocacy*, p. 6.

36. Swerdlow, *Presidential Debates: 1988 and Beyond*, p. 156.

37. Minow and Sloan, *For Great Debates*, p. 20.

38. Lanoue and Schrott, *Joint Press Conference*, p. 18.

39. Helllweg, Pfau, and Brydon, *Televised Presidential Debates: Advocacy*, p. 6.

40. Lanoue and Schrott, *Joint Press Conference*, p. 18.

41. "The Blooper Heard Round the World," *Time*, October 18, 1976, p. 13, cited in ibid., p. 19.

42. Thomas E. Patterson, *The Mass Media Election: How Americans Choose Their President* (New York: Praeger, 1980), p. 125.

43. Frederick T. Steeper, "Public Response to Gerald Ford's Statements on Eastern Europe in the Second Debate," in George F. Bishop, Robert G. Meadow, and Marilyn Jackson-Beeck, eds., *The Presidential Debates: Media, Electoral, and Policy Perspectives* (New York: Praeger, 1978), p. 101.

44. Quoted in Minow and Sloan, *For Great Debates*, p. 20.

45. Robert V. Friedenberg, "Patterns and Trends in National Political Debates: 1960–1988," in Robert V. Friedenberg, ed., *Rhetorical Studies of National Political Debates 1960–1988* (New York: Praeger, 1990), p. 188.

46. Swerdlow, *Presidential Debates: 1988 and Beyond*, p. 156.

47. Lanoue and Schrott, *Joint Press Conference*, p. 23.

48. Ibid.; Minow and Sloan, *For Great Debates*, p. 22.

49. Quoted in Minow and Sloan, *For Great Debates*, p. 21.

50. Gerald Pomper, "The Presidential Election," in Gerald M. Pomper et al., *The Election of 1980: Reports and Interpretations* (Chatham, N.J.: Chatham House Publishers, 1981), p. 75.

51. Joel L. Swerdlow, *Beyond Debate: A Paper on Televised Presidential Debates* (New York: Twentieth Century Fund, 1984), p. 5.

52. Ibid., pp. 37–38.

53. Ibid., p. 38; Albert Cantril, "The Polls Shouldn't Govern the Debate," *New York Times*, September 7, 1980, p. E19; Peter Hart, "The League Passes the Buck," *Washington Post*, August 22, 1980, p. A15.

54. Minow and Sloan, *For Great Debates*, p. 26.

55. Kathleen A. Frankovic, "Public Opinion Trends," in Pomper et al., *Election of 1980*, pp. 106–7.

56. Pomper, "Presidential Election," p. 80.

57. Frankovic, "Public Opinion Trends," p. 108.

58. Swerdlow, *Beyond Debate*, p. 10. Nielsen Media Research estimated that as many as 55.4 million households, or 150 million persons, watched the debate (Swerdlow, *Presidential Debates: 1988 and Beyond*, p. 159).

59. Lanoue and Schrott, *Joint Press Conference*, p. 28.

60. Quoted in Minow and Sloan, *For Great Debates*, p. 26.

61. Paul R. Abramson, John H. Aldrich, and David W. Rohde, *Change and Continuity in the 1980 Elections* (Washington, D.C.: Congressional Quarterly, 1982), p. 45.

62. Lanoue and Schrott, *Joint Press Conference*, pp. 30–31.

63. Swerdlow, *Beyond Debate*, p. 11.

64. Henry Geller, *Federal Communications Commission*, 54 P. & F. Radio Reg. 2d 1246 (1983).

65. Neale, *Campaign Debates in Presidential General Elections*, p. 6.

66. Minow and Sloan, *For Great Debates*, p. 32.

67. Kraus, *Televised Presidential Debates and Public Policy*, p. 57.

68. Minow and Sloan, *For Great Debates*, p. 32.

69. Ibid., p. 31. According to the Nielsen organization, the audience was even larger. Its statistics estimate that the debate was watched in 50.2 million households, representing about 132 million persons. See Swerdlow, *Presidential Debates: 1988 and Beyond*, p. 163.

70. Neale, *Campaign Debates in Presidential General Elections*, p. 6.

71. Lanoue and Schrott, *Joint Press Conference*, p. 34.

72. Neale, *Campaign Debates in Presidential General Elections*, p. 7.

73. Lanoue and Schrott, *Joint Press Conference*, p. 36.

74. See, for example, David J. Lanoue and Peter R. Schrott, "Voters' Reactions to Televised Presidential Debates: Measurement of the Source and Magnitude of Opinion Change," *Political Psychology* 10, no. 2 (1989): 275–85.

75. Minow and Sloan, *For Great Debates*, p. 32.

76. Commission on National Elections, *Electing the President: A Program for Reform* (Washington, D.C.: Center for Strategic and International Studies, 1986), pp. 41–44.

77. Ibid., p. 44.

78. Minow and Sloan, *For Great Debates*, p. 36.

79. Ibid., p. 38. An earlier Twentieth Century Fund study of the debates process had reached a similar conclusion. In 1979, the first Twentieth Century Fund Task Force Report on Televised Presidential Debates concluded that "presidential debates should become a regular and customary feature of the presidential election campaign" and suggested that this could be accomplished by "creating conditions which will encourage candidates to participate and broadcasters to provide coverage." A key to this process, the Task Force noted, would be to ensure "that a nonprofit, nonpartisan citizen group devoted to citizen education and participation should act as sponsor" (see *With the Nation Watching*, pp. 5–6).

80. For a brief discussion of the Commission's formation, see the statement of Frank Fahrenkopf, cochairman, Commission on Presidential Debates, in *Presidential Debates*, hearings before the Subcommittee on Elections, U.S. Congress, House, Committee on House Administration, 103d Cong., 1st sess., June 17, 1993, pp. 31–35.

81. Hellweg, Pfau, and Brydon, *Televised Presidential Debates: Advocacy*, p. 10.

82. Ibid.

83. Jack W. Germond and Jules Witcover, *Whose Broad Stripes and Bright Stars? The Trivial Pursuit of the Presidency 1988* (New York: Warner Books, 1989), pp. 425–27. See also Jack W. Germond and Jules Witcover, *Mad as*

Hell: Revolt at the Ballot Box, 1992 (New York: Warner Books, 1993), pp. 464–68.

84. Hellweg, Pfau, and Brydon, *Televised Presidential Debates: Advocacy*, p. 11. For a description of the negotiations, see Germond and Witcover, *Whose Broad Stripes and Bright Stars?*, pp. 426–29; Peter Goldman and Tom Mathews, *The Quest for the Presidency 1988* (New York: Simon & Schuster, 1989), pp. 371–73.

85. Hellweg, Pfau, and Brydon, *Televised Presidential Debates: Advocacy*, p. 11.

86. Neale, *Campaign Debates in Presidential General Elections*, p. 10.

87. Paul R. Abramson, John H. Aldrich, and David W. Rohde, *Change and Continuity in the 1988 Elections* (Washington, D.C.: Congressional Quarterly, 1990), p. 48.

88. Quoted in Neale, *Campaign Debates in Presidential General Elections*, p. 9.

89. Quoted in Abramson, Aldrich, and Rohde, *Change and Continuity in the 1988 Elections*, p. 48.

90. Lanoue and Schrott, *Joint Press Conference*, p. 38.

91. Abramson, Aldrich, and Rohde, *Change and Continuity in the 1988 Elections*, p. 48; Thomas B. Rosenstiel, "Ringside Media Give Split Decision," *Los Angeles Times*, September 26, 1988, p. A13; Barbara G. Farah and Ethel Klein, "Public Opinion Trends," in Gerald M. Pomper et al., *The Elections of 1988: Reports and Interpretations* (Chatham, N.J.: Chatham House Publishers, 1989), p. 107.

92. Diana Prentice Carlin, "Presidential Debates as Focal Points for Campaign Arguments," *Political Communication* 9, no. 4 (October/December 1992): 258.

93. Abramson, Aldrich, and Rohde, *Change and Continuity in the 1988 Elections*, p. 49.

94. Carlin, "Presidential Debates as Focal Points," p. 261.

95. Lanoue and Schrott, *Joint Press Conference*, p. 41.

96. Ibid.; Carlin, "Presidential Debates as Focal Points," p. 262.

97. Abramson, Aldrich, and Rohde, *Change and Continuity in the 1988 Elections*, p. 50; Lanoue and Schrott, *Joint Press Conference*, p. 41.

98. James B. Lemert, "Do Televised Presidential Debates Help Inform Voters?" *Journal of Broadcasting and Electronic Media* 37, no. 1 (Winter 1993): 83–94; David J. Lanoue, "The 'Turning Point': Viewers' Reactions to the Second 1988 Presidential Debate," *American Politics Quarterly* 19, no. 1 (January 1991): 80–95.

99. Times Mirror Center for the People and the Press, "The People, the Press & Politics: Campaign '92—Voters Say 'Thumbs Up' to Campaign, Process, & Coverage," survey no. 13, Washington, D.C., November 15, 1992, p. 1.

100. Diana Prentice Carlin et al., "The Effects of Presidential Debate Formats on Clash: A Comparative Analysis," *Argumentation and Advocacy* 27 (Winter 1991): 126–36.

CHAPTER TWO

1. Commission on Presidential Debates, "'Debates '92': A Symposium," Washington, D.C., May 9, 1990. A transcript of the symposium proceedings is available from the Commission.

2. Statement of Paul Kirk, cochairman, Commission on Presidential Debates, in *Presidential Debates*, hearings before the Subcommittee on Elections, U.S. Congress, House, Committee on House Administration, 103d Cong., 1st sess., June 17, 1993, p. 92.

3. Statement of Frank Fahrenkopf, cochairman, Commission on Presidential Debates, in ibid., pp. 35–36.

4. Ibid., p. 36.

5. Quoted in B. Drummond Ayres, Jr., "Networks Seek Presidential Debate Overhaul," *New York Times*, September 26, 1991, p. A22.

6. For a discussion of the proposal, see testimony of Martin Plissner, political director, CBS News, in *Presidential Debates*, hearings before the Subcommittee on Elections, pp. 111–16; Thomas H. Neale, *Campaign Debates in Presidential General Elections* (Washington, D.C.: Congressional Research Service, June 1993), pp. 12–14.

7. Neale, *Campaign Debates in Presidential General Elections*, p. 13; Howard Kurtz and Dan Balz, "Bipartisan Panel Rejects Debate Proposal by Networks," *Washington Post*, September 26, 1991, p. A14.

8. Testimony of Plissner, in *Presidential Debates*, hearings before the Subcommittee on Elections, p. 111.

9. Ibid.

10. Ayres, "Networks Seek Presidential Debate Overhaul." The first quote is from the League and the second from Ayres's text.

11. See testimony of Plissner, in *Presidential Debates*, hearings before the Subcommittee on Elections, p. 111; John W. Mashek, "Impasse Threatens Campaign Debates," *Boston Globe*, May 30, 1992, p. 8; Thomas B. Rosenstiel, "Presidential Debate Talks Break Down," *Los Angeles Times*, May 30, 1992, p. A15.

12. Rosenstiel, "Presidential Debate Talks Break Down"; "Debate over Television Debates," *Washington Post*, June 7, 1992, p. A22.

13. Quoted in Kurtz and Balz, "Bipartisan Panel Rejects Debate Proposal." See also Paul G. Kirk, Jr., and Frank J. Fahrenkopf, Jr., "Debates and the Networks' Role," *Washington Post*, October 27, 1991, p. C7. For a response to their argument see Martin Plissner, "Debates: You Can Trust the Networks," *Washington Post*, November 5, 1991, p. A21.

14. Quoted in Ayres, "Networks Seek Presidential Debate Overhaul."

15. The two studies that formed the impetus for the creation of the Commission on Presidential Debates both voiced concerns about the propriety of network sponsorship of debates in light of their role in covering these events. As a result, they recommended the establishment of a bipartisan, independent organization to serve as debate sponsor, noting that this

RHODES COLLEGE BOOKSTORE-STUDENT CENTER
OPEN MON-WED 8:30-6, THUR-FRI 8:30-4.
PHONE 901-726-3535, FAX 901-726-3819

23-SEP-1996 17:58:22 96092303 EVENING

FOTOFOLIO/POSTCARDS   N
            2 @ $ 0.38 $ 0.76
LET AMERICA DECIDE (P)   N $ 9.95

              Subtotal $ 10.71
                   TAX $ 0.06
                 Total $ 10.77

                  CASH $ 21.00
       Amount Tendered $ 21.00
                Change $ 10.23

Welcome Class of 2000 ! The Bookstore
is NOW OPEN TIL 6PM, MONDAY-WEDNESDAY !
We will be open Saturday, Oct. 5th, 11-2.

Welcome Class of 2000 ! The Bookstore
is NOW OPEN TIL 6PM, MONDAY-WEDNESDAY !
We will be open Saturday, Oct. 5th, 11-4.

approach would also better ensure the institutionalization of presidential debates. See Commission on National Elections, *Electing the President: A Program for Reform* (Washington, D.C.: Center for Strategic and International Studies, 1986), pp. 41–44; Newton N. Minow and Clifford M. Sloan, *For Great Debates: A New Plan for Future Presidential TV Debates* (New York: Priority Press, 1987), pp. 37–38.

16. Plissner, "Debates: You Can Trust the Networks."

17. Kurtz and Balz, "Bipartisan Panel Rejects Debate Proposal"; Rosenstiel, "Presidential Debate Talks Break Down."

18. Commission on Presidential Debates, "Commission on Presidential Debates Announces 1992 Plans, Releases Candidate Selection Criteria," press release, Washington, D.C., June 11, 1992.

19. Commission on Presidential Debates, "Commission on Presidential Debates' Candidate Selection Criteria for 1992 General Election Debate Participation," Washington, D.C., resolution adopted June 4, 1992.

20. Statement of Frank Fahrenkopf in *Presidential Debates*, hearings before the Subcommittee on Elections, pp. 36–37.

21. Cited in the testimony of Bobby R. Burchfield, general counsel of the Bush reelection committee, in *Presidential Debates*, hearings before the Subcommittee on Elections, pp. 45–46.

22. For example, in an August 17 interview with CNN, President Bush said, "There will be debates. But whether it's going to be three or what number, we have not decided what we want." See "Bush Accepts Debates, Subject to Negotiations," *New York Times*, August 18, 1992, p. A11. See also Thomas Oliphant, "Baker Moves to Make the Debates More Comfy for Bush," *Boston Globe*, August 30, 1992, p. 67.

23. B. Drummond Ayres, Jr., "Bush Rejects Panel's Plan for 3 Debates," *New York Times*, September 4, 1992, p. A13; John W. Mashek, "Bush Bars Plan for 3 Debates, Lone Moderator," *Boston Globe*, September 4, 1992, p. 1.

24. Testimony of Burchfield in *Presidential Debates*, hearings before the Subcommittee on Elections, p. 45.

25. Cited in ibid., p. 47.

26. These statements are from Mickey Kantor's prepared statement in response to the Bush campaign's formal rejection of the Commission plan as quoted in Ayres, "Bush Rejects Panel's Plan for 3 Debates."

27. Jack W. Germond and Jules Witcover, *Mad as Hell: Revolt at the Ballot Box, 1992* (New York: Warner Books, 1993), pp. 468–70. See also Richard L. Berke, "First TV Debate Canceled as Bush Sticks to Objections over Format," *New York Times*, September 17, 1992, p. A1; "'Chickens' Haunting Bush at Rallies," *New York Times*, September 26, 1992, p. A6.

28 Gwen Ifill, "Where Debate Was to Be, Clinton Shows Up for Rally," *New York Times*, September 23, 1992, p. A21.

29. Quoted in Richard L. Berke, "Bush Shifts Stand, Saying He's Ready to Hold 4 Debates," *New York Times*, September 30, 1992, p. A1.

30. Berke, "First TV Debate Canceled."

31. Richard L. Berke, "Bush Camp Gives Ultimatum on Debates," *New York Times*, September 15, 1992, p. A22.

32. Thomas B. Edsall, "Bush Rejects Scheduling of Debate," *Washington Post*, September 23, 1992, p. A12. See also "How He Won," *Newsweek*, special election issue, November/December 1992, p. 85. One report also claimed that Baker did not want debates to become "institutionalized—that is, have them reach a stature that a candidate would be obliged to participate, and under rigid conditions not agreed to by him, when it might not be to his political advantage to do so" (Germond and Witcover, *Mad as Hell*, p. 464).

33. Ifill, "Where Debate Was to Be, Clinton Shows."

34. Berke, "Bush Shifts Stand," p. A22.

35. This poll was conducted from September 22 to 24 and is available through the NEXIS RPOLL file.

36. Reported in Edsall, "Bush Rejects Rescheduling of Debate."

37. The findings of this research are reported in the testimony of Diana Carlin, associate professor of communications, University of Kansas, in *Presidential Debates*, hearings before the Subcommittee on Elections, pp. 148–53.

38. Berke, "Bush Shifts Stand," p. A1. One Bush associate explained the decision to issue a proposal as follows: "We had to do it. Otherwise, we would lose the election. We were stuck at 40 percent for Bush and 50 percent for Clinton in the polls, and we figured in the last week that Bush would lose by something like 52–48 unless we did something." (Quoted in Michael Kranish, "Aides to Bush, Clinton Discuss Debate Plans," *Boston Globe*, October 1, 1992, p. 19.)

39. For a more detailed discussion of the particulars of the negotiations from the perspective of the participants, see the testimony of Burchfield and of Harold Ickes, former deputy chair, Democratic National Committee, in *Presidential Debates*, hearings before the Subcommittee on Elections, pp. 41–68.

40. Germond and Witcover report that Clinton asked Kantor to suggest a town-meeting format in a telephone call that took place during a break in the negotiations. See *Mad as Hell*, p. 472.

41. Testimony of Burchfield in *Presidential Debates*, hearings before the Subcommittee on Elections, p. 50.

42. Ibid.

43. As in previous elections, this provision led some journalists and news organizations to announce their decision not to participate if selected. See Howard Kurtz, "Journalists Posing Debate Questions to Be Chosen by Bush, Clinton Camps," *Washington Post*, October 4, 1992, p. A23; Richard L. Berke, "Debate on Debates Over, Debate on Panel Begins," *New York Times*, October 6, 1992, p. A15.

44. This description was reported by CNN as cited in Keith Darren Eisner,

"Non-Major Party Candidates and Televised Presidential Debates: The Merits of Legislative Inclusion," *University of Pennsylvania Law Review* 141, no. 3 (January 1993): 1024–25.

45. The Commission's decision to invite Perot to all three presidential debates came only after an initial decision to invite him to just the first debate was rejected by the Bush and Clinton camps. On October 6, the Commission sent a letter to the two major-party campaign chairs accepting the invitation to sponsor the debates "subject to [certain] conditions and understandings." One of these conditions was that Perot and Stockdale be invited to the October 11 and October 13 forums, with a determination about Perot's participation in the last two debates to be made after these meetings. Should the Commission decide to exclude Perot from the last two forums, the campaigns would reserve the right to seek an alternative sponsor. The campaigns responded that this piecemeal approach was unacceptable. The Commission then reconsidered its position and issued its October 7 letter inviting Perot to participate in all of the proposed debates. For a recounting of these events, see testimony of Burchfield in *Presidential Debates*, hearings before the Subcommittee on Elections, pp. 51–52.

46. Edward M. Fouhy, "The Debates: A Winning Miniseries," *Washington Journalism Review*, December 1992, p. 27.

47. Ibid., p. 28.

48. "The Aftermath of Round Three," *Congressional Quarterly Weekly Report*, October 24, 1992, p. 3336.

49. Ronald D. Elving, "Clinton's Lead Holds Steady; Bush Fails to Galvanize," *Congressional Quarterly Weekly Report*, October 17, 1992, p. 3275.

50. Testimony of Kathleen Hall Jamieson, professor, Annenberg School for Communication, University of Pennsylvania, in *Presidential Debates*, hearings before the Subcommittee on Elections, p. 105.

51. Fouhy, "The Debates: A Winning Miniseries," p. 27. See also the remarks of Carole Simpson in Commission on Presidential Debates, "Review of 1992 Presidential Debates," Washington, D.C., May 4, 1993, p. 10. A copy of the transcript of this symposium is available from the Commission.

52. Neale, *Campaign Debates in Presidential General Elections*, p. 14.

53. See, for example, Richard L. Berke, "Which Debate System Worked Best? It's a Debate," *New York Times*, October 21, 1992, p. A19.

54. Quoted in Paul R. Abramson, John H. Aldrich, and David W. Rohde, *Change and Continuity in the 1992 Elections* (Washington, D.C.: Congressional Quarterly Press, 1994), p. 61.

55. Quoted in Berke, "Which Debate System Worked Best?"

56. The wordings of the questions are based on the transcripts published in the *New York Times*, October 12, 1992 (pp. A14–17), October 16, 1992 (pp. A11–14), and October 20, 1992 (pp. A20–23).

57. Berke, "Which Debate System Worked Best?" See also Charles Krauthammer, "Little Lessons of the Campaign," *Washington Post*, October 23, 1992, p. A21.

58. Ibid.

59. Ibid.

60. David S. Broder and Guy Gugliotta, "Quayle and Gore Exchange Broadsides," *Washington Post*, October 14, 1992, p. A14.

61. Times Mirror Center for the People and the Press, "The People, the Press & Politics: Campaign '92—Voters Say 'Thumbs Up' to Campaign, Process, & Coverage," survey no. 13, Washington, D.C., November 15, 1992, p. 1.

62. Ibid.

63. Andrew Kohut, director, Times Mirror Center for the People and the Press, in *Presidential Debates*, hearings before the Subcommittee on Elections, p. 68.

64. Times Mirror Center for the People and the Press, "The People, the Press & Politics," p. 1.

65. Testimony of Kohut in *Presidential Debates*, hearings before the Subcommittee on Elections, p. 71.

66. Ronald Elving observed that "Clinton also gained an advantage [in the second debate] by letting Bush and Perot speak ahead of him on nine of the audience's 13 questions" ("Clinton's Lead Holds Steady," p. 3275).

67. Kathleen A. Frankovic, "Public Opinion in the 1992 Campaign," in Gerald Pomper et al., *The Election of 1992: Reports and Interpretations* (Chatham, N.J.: Chatham House Publishers, 1993), p. 120.

68. Thomas B. Rosenstiel, "Instant Polls Pick Winner while Debate Still Echoes," *Los Angeles Times*, October 13, 1992, p. A14.

69. Frankovic, "Public Opinion in the 1992 Campaign," p. 119.

70. See Elving, "Clinton's Lead Holds Steady," pp. 3274-75; "The Aftermath of Round Three," p. 3336.

71. Elving, "Clinton's Lead Holds Steady," p. 3274.

72. Neale, *Campaign Debates in Presidential General Elections*, p. 15.

73. David S. Broder, "Strong Showing by Bush May Change Little," *Washington Post*, October 20, 1992, p. Al.

74. "The Aftermath of Round Three," p. 3336.

75. Ibid.; Elving, "Clinton's Lead Holds Steady."

76. Times Mirror Center for the People and the Press, "The People, the Press & Politics," p. 13.

CHAPTER THREE

1. See, among others, *With the Nation Watching: Report of the Twentieth Century Fund Task Force on Televised Presidential Debates* (Lexington, Mass.: D. C. Heath and Company, 1979); Joel L. Swerdlow, *Beyond Debate: A Paper on Televised Presidential Debates* (New York: Twentieth Century Fund, 1984); Newton N. Minow and Clifford M. Sloan, *For Great Debates: A New Plan for*

Future Presidential TV Debates (New York: Priority Press, 1987); Commission on Presidential Debates, "'Debates '92': A Symposium," Washington, D.C., May 9, 1990; Kathleen Hall Jamieson and David S. Birdsell, *Presidential Debates: The Challenge of Creating an Informed Electorate* (New York: Oxford University Press, 1988). Former presidential candidate John B. Anderson has suggested an even more extensive series of debates in *A Proper Institution: Guaranteeing Televised Presidential Debates* (New York: Priority Press, 1988).

2. For a complete timetable of modern presidential and vice presidential debates, see Jamieson and Birdsell, *Presidential Debates: The Challenge*, Appendix 1; Thomas H. Neale, *Campaign Debates in Presidential General Elections* (Washington, D.C.: Congressional Research Service, June 1993), pp. 16–17.

3. The 1960 debates were the major exception. Each candidate was allowed an eight-minute opening statement in the first and fourth debates.

4. Some academic studies have challenged this criticism of the press panel format. These studies demonstrate that the format, despite its shortcomings, has provided notable contrast and clash between the candidates. See Diana Prentice Carlin et al., "The Effects of Presidential Debate Formats on Clash: A Comparative Analysis," *Argumentation and Advocacy* 27 (Winter 1991): 126–36; Diana Prentice Carlin, "Presidential Debates as Focal Points for Campaign Arguments," *Political Communication* 9, no. 4 (October/December 1992): 251–65.

5. For a thorough listing of the advantages of a series of debates, see Swerdlow, *Beyond Debate*, pp. 15–18.

6. Ibid., p. 15.

7. Thomason's role is reported by Bobby Burchfield, general counsel of the Bush reelection committee, in *Presidential Debates*, hearings before the Subcommittee on Elections, U.S. Congress, House, Committee on House Administration, 103d Cong., 1st sess., June 17, 1993, p. 49. See also Jack W. Germond and Jules Witcover, *Mad as Hell: Revolt at the Ballot Box, 1992* (New York: Warner Books, 1993), p. 480.

8. See Harold Ickes, former deputy chair, Democratic National Committee, in *Presidential Debates*, hearings before the Subcommittee on Elections, p. 64; Bobby Burchfield in Commission on Presidential Debates, "Review of 1992 Presidential Debates," Washington, D.C., May 4, 1993, p. 58.

9. See, for example, Edward M. Fouhy, "The Debates: A Winning Miniseries," *Washington Journalism Review*, December 1992, p. 27; Carole Simpson in Commission on Presidential Debates, "Review of 1992 Presidential Debates," p. 10.

10. Commission on Presidential Debates, "Review of 1992 Presidential Debates," p. 12.

11. Ibid., p. 10.

12. In a recent congressional hearing on the issue of presidential debates, William O. Wheatley, the executive producer of the Brokaw Report for NBC

News, said that "a longer period would have eliminated some of the scheduling conflicts with televised professional sports, conflicts that in 1992 resulted in several debates being held in early prime time in the East, denying some West Coast viewers the opportunity to see the debates as they happened" (*Presidential Debates*, hearings before the Subcommittee on Elections, p. 118). In the same hearing, Kathleen Hall Jamieson, professor at the Annenberg School for Communication, University of Pennsylvania, observed that "when we are airing debates at times that exclude most of those on the West Coast who have not yet gotten home or are driving home, we are not acting responsibly" (*Presidential Debates*, hearings before the Subcommittee on Elections, p. 104).

13. Ibid., p. 18.

14. These focus groups were conducted by members of the Speech Communication Association, a professional academic organization, in 17 cities in 16 states. Overall, 62 focus groups were conducted involving 624 participants. See Commission on Presidential Debates, "Review of 1992 Presidential Debates," pp. 23–36, especially p. 28. Joel Swerdlow has also said that an early debate would play a valuable role in setting the tone of the campaign and allowing the candidates to begin to present their views. See *Beyond Debate*, p. 16.

15. Commission on Presidential Debates, "'Debates '92,'" p. 19.

16. Transcripts of the 1988 debates are taken from the *New York Times*, September 26, 1988 (pp. A16–19), October 6, 1988 (pp. B20–23), and October 14, 1988 (pp. A14–17). Transcripts of the 1992 debates are from the *New York Times*, October 12, 1992 (pp. A11–14), and October 20, 1992 (pp. A20–23).

17. Ibid., p. 14.

18. Commission on Presidential Debates, "Review of 1992 Presidential Debates," p. 26.

19. Susan A. Hellweg, Michael Pfau, and Steven R. Brydon, *Televised Presidential Debates: Advocacy in Contemporary America* (New York: Praeger, 1992), p. 126.

20. Commission on Presidential Debates, "Review of 1992 Presidential Debates," p. 14.

21. Testimony of Jamieson in *Presidential Debates*, hearings before the Subcommittee on Elections, p. 108; Fay S. Joyce, "Bush View of His Charge," *New York Times*, October 19, 1984, p. A17.

22. Hellweg, Pfau, and Brydon, *Televised Presidential Debates*, pp. 23–24.

23. Jamieson and Birdsell, *Presidential Debates: The Challenge*, p. 201.

24. Ibid., p. 202.

25. Swerdlow, *Beyond Debate*, p. 20.

26. Jamieson and Birdsell, *Presidential Debates: The Challenge*, p. 204.

27. Commission on Presidential Debates, "Review of 1992 Presidential Debates," pp. 26–27.

28. Ibid., p. 27.

29. See *With the Nation Watching*, p. 102; the remarks of Jamieson and Hal Bruno, director of political coverage, ABC News, in *Presidential Debates*, hearings before the Subcommittee on Elections, pp. 104 and 181, respectively.

30. These remarks are taken from a videotape of the debate since remarks to the audience are deleted from most published transcripts.

31. See, for example, John W. Mashek, "Democrats Had Cheerleaders at Bentsen–Quayle Debate, Says Adviser," *Boston Globe*, May 10, 1990, p. 6.

CHAPTER FOUR

1. The San Diego site had to be scrapped because the tight schedule agreed to by the candidates did not allow time for cross-country travel. The Bush campaign resisted the selection of Louisville as a site because of its concern about the political damage it had endured there as a result of the events surrounding the cancellation of the Commission's proposed Louisville debate, which included a rally attended by Clinton and negative editorial opinion. See Michael K. Frisby, "Highly-Focused Debate Plan Is Seen," *Boston Globe*, October 3, 1992, p. 6.

2. See the testimonies of Arthur Block, special counsel to the New Alliance Party, and Stuart Reges, national director of the Libertarian Party, in *Presidential Debates*, hearings before the Subcommittee on Elections, U.S. Congress, House, Committee on House Administration, 103d Cong., 1st sess., June 17, 1993, pp. 137 and 162–63.

3. Testimony of Harold Ickes, former deputy chair, Democratic National Committee, in ibid., p. 66.

4. Sander Vanocur in Commission on Presidential Debates, "Review of 1992 Presidential Debates," Washington, D.C., May 4, 1993, p. 6.

5. Testimony of Newton Minow, former chair, Federal Communications Commission, in *Presidential Debates*, hearings before the Subcommittee on Elections, p. 194.

6. Testimony of Bobby Burchfield, general counsel of the Bush reelection committee, in ibid., p. 51.

7. Testimony of Martin Plissner, political director, CBS News, in ibid., p. 112.

8. Quoted in Leslie Phillips, "Debates: Big Effort, but Little Progress," *USA Today*, October 1, 1992, p. 12A.

9. Brady Williamson in Commission on Presidential Debates, "Review of the 1992 Presidential Debates," p. 59.

10. In a symposium on debates held after the 1992 election, Commission on Presidential Debates cochair Frank Fahrenkopf observed: "I think the important thing to remember here is that, at least on the Republican side, Jim Baker had felt—and I think rightfully so—that in negotiating the debate agreement of 1984 with Mondale people and negotiating the debate format

in 1988 with Governor Dukakis's people, they had cleaned their clocks, they'd gotten everything that they wanted, and there was no desire to have anybody at the table but the opposition [in 1992]—hopeful that they could do the same thing again" (Commission on Presidential Debates, "Review of 1992 Presidential Debates," pp. 44–45). See also Jack W. Germond and Jules Witcover, *Whose Broad Stripes and Bright Stars? The Trivial Pursuit of the Presidency 1988* (New York: Warner Books, 1989), pp. 425–27.

11. See, among others, R. W. Apple, Jr., "Quayle on the Offensive," *New York Times*, October 14, 1992, p. A1; Mary McGrory, "Quayle on the Offensive," *Washington Post*, October 15, 1992, p. A2; Scot Lehigh, "VP Bested Expectations, Not Foe," *Boston Globe*, October 14, 1992, p. 1.

12. Quoted in Richard L. Berke, "Which Debate System Worked Best? It's a Debate," *New York Times*, October 21, 1992, p. A19.

13. *With the Nation Watching: Report of the Twentieth Century Fund Task Force on Televised Presidential Debates* (Lexington, Mass.: D. C. Heath and Company, 1979), p. 90.

14. Susan E. Spotts, "Recent Developments: The Presidential Debates Act of 1992," *Harvard Journal on Legislation* 29 (Summer 1992): 561.

15. Joel L. Swerdlow, *Beyond Debate: A Paper on Televised Presidential Debates* (New York: Twentieth Century Fund, 1984), p. 3.

16. See, for example, the views of Dan Rather and Ted Koppel as reported in Berke, "Which Debate System Worked Best?" See also David J. Lanoue and Peter R. Schrott, *The Joint Press Conference: The History, Impact, and Prospects of American Presidential Debates* (Westport, Conn.: Greenwood Press, 1991).

17. See Commission on Presidential Debates, "Review of 1992 Presidential Debates," pp. 21–36.

18. Ibid., p. 25.

19. See the statements by Burchfield and Ickes in *Presidential Debates*, hearing before the Subcommittee on Elections, pp. 59 and 65–66.

20. Author's interview with Lane Venardos, New York, May 27, 1994.

21. Paul Kirk, cochair of the Commission, noted "that the Commission never felt and does not now feel that its proposals are dictates to any campaign. . . . [W]e chose our dates and our calendar accordingly and selected sites accordingly, knowing that the campaigns might have a difference of opinion, that there would be dialogue. But we felt, having come through 1988, you have to start from somewhere and to put a blueprint out there that people can talk about" (Commission on Presidential Debates, "Review of 1992 Presidential Debates," p. 43). According to Bobby Burchfield, the Commission's debate plan "wasn't the only proposal, nor was it intended, I think, by . . . the Commission, to be the only proposal that was to be considered" (ibid.).

22. Testimony of Ickes in *Presidential Debates*, hearings before the Subcommittee on Elections, p. 65.

23. Bobby Burchfield in Commission of Presidential Debates, "Review of 1992 Presidential Debates," p. 43.

24. Newton N. Minow and Clifford M. Sloan, *For Great Debates: A New Plan for Future Presidential TV Debates* (New York: Priority Press, 1987), p. 37. For an alternative view, see Tom Brokaw, "Networks Should Sponsor Debates," in Joel L. Swerdlow, ed., *Presidential Debates: 1988 and Beyond* (Washington, D.C.: Congressional Quarterly, 1987).

25. Swerdlow, *Beyond Debate*, p. 50.

26. The Freedom Forum Media Studies Center, *The Finish Line: Covering the Campaign's Final Days* (New York: Freedom Forum Media Studies Center, January 1993), p. 40.

27. Swerdlow, *Beyond Debate*, p. 50.

28. See Minow and Sloan, *For Great Debates*, pp. 37–39; Newton N. Minow and Clifford M. Sloan, "Political Parties Should Sponsor Debates," in Swerdlow, ed., *Presidential Debates: 1988 and Beyond*.

29. Hal Bruno, for example, has declared: "I believe, and I've advocated this for some time, that maybe it's up to the parties to discipline the candidates, that it should be maybe party rule at the convention, rather than federal law, but a party law, that if you accept the nomination of the party, you will agree that you will take part—you and your ticket—will take part in four debates in the general election" (Commission on Presidential Debates, "Review of 1992 Presidential Debates," p. 7).

30. Swerdlow, *Beyond Debate*, p. 53.

CHAPTER FIVE

1. Kathleen Hall Jamieson, "The Subversive Effects of a Focus on Strategy in News Coverage of Presidential Campaigns," in *1-800-PRESIDENT: The Report of the Twentieth Century Fund Task Force on Television and the Campaign of 1992* (New York: The Twentieth Century Fund Press, 1993), p. 41. Jamieson develops this argument at greater length in *Dirty Politics: Deception, Distraction, and Democracy* (New York: Oxford University Press, 1992).

2. Jamieson, "The Subversive Effects of a Focus on Strategy."

3. This description of the ABC poll is based on the discussion in David J. Lanoue and Peter R. Schrott, *The Joint Press Conference: The History, Impact, and Prospects of American Presidential Debates* (Westport, Conn.: Greenwood Press, 1991), p. 29.

4. Debra Gersh, "Improving the Presidential Debates," *Editor and Publisher*, April 24, 1993, p. 40.

5. Ibid.

6. Cited in Wendy Zeligson Adler, "The Debates: The Day After," in The Freedom Forum Media Studies Center, *The Finish Line: Covering the Campaign's Final Days* (New York: Freedom Forum Media Studies Center, January 1993), p. 37.

7. Quoted in Gersh, "Improving the Presidential Debates," p. 40.

8. Testimony of Kathleen Hall Jamieson, professor, Annenberg School for Communication, University of Pennsylvania, in *Presidential Debates*, hearings before the Subcommittee on Elections, U.S. Congress, House, Committee on House Administration, 103d Cong., 1st sess., June 17, 1993, p. 107.

9. The Freedom Forum Media Studies Center, *Finish Line*, p. 14. The newspapers included in this study were the *New York Times, Washington Post, Miami Herald, Los Angeles Times, Chicago Tribune,* and *Austin American-Statesman.*

10. Ibid., p. 36.

11. Wayne Jacques et al., "Some Aspects of Major Newspaper Coverage of the 1992 Presidential Debates," *American Behavioral Scientist* 37, no. 2 (November 1993): 255. The newspapers included in this study were the *New York Times, Washington Post, Chicago Tribune, Los Angeles Times,* and *Wall Street Journal.*

12. Ibid., pp. 255–56.

13. See Adler, "The Debates: The Day After"; Dale Russakoff and Richard Morin, "Watching the Debates, Looking for Someone to Believe In," *Washington Post,* October 21, 1992, p. A21; Doug Payne, "Undecided Voters Unswayed by Debate," *Atlanta Constitution,* October 16, 1992, p. A7.

14. Adler, "The Debates: The Day After," pp. 36–44.

15. There was some use of instant polling analyses in the 1988 debate coverage. See Andrew Rosenthal, "Third TV Debate Brings Change in Commentary," *New York Times,* October 15, 1988, p. A8; Gregory Katz, "Meter Gives Slight Victory to Dukakis," *USA Today,* October 14, 1988, p. 6A.

16. Michael X. Delli Carpini, Robert D. Holsworth, and Scott Keeter, "'Consumer Journalism' in the Electronic Age: Instant Reaction to the 'People's' Presidential Debate," in The Freedom Forum Media Studies Center, *Finishing Line,* pp. 47–48.

17. Ibid., p. 47.

18. Ibid., p. 48.

19. Mark Thalhimer, "The Debate Pulse: Rapid-Response, Interactive Polling," in The Freedom Forum Media Studies Center, *Finishing Line,* pp. 50–51.

20. Ibid., p. 51.

21. Delli Carpini, Holsworth, and Keeter, "'Consumer Journalism' in the Electronic Age," p. 51.

22. Ibid., pp. 52–53.

23. Jamieson, "The Subversive Effects of a Focus on Strategy," p. 47.

CHAPTER SIX

1. Testimony of Harold Ickes, former deputy chair, Democratic National Committee, *Presidential Debates*, hearings before the Subcommittee on Elections, U.S. Congress, House, Committee on House Administration, 103d Cong., 1st sess., June 17, 1993, pp. 66–67.

2. Beverly Lindsey in Commission on Presidential Debates, "Review of 1992 Presidential Debates," Washington, D.C., May 4, 1993, p. 47.

3. Bobby Burchfield in ibid., p. 41.

4. This remark was made in a symposium on debates held after the 1988 election. See Commission on Presidential Debates, "'Debates '92': A Symposium," Washington, D.C., May 9, 1990, p. 32. See also Jack W. Germond and Jules Witcover, "Are Presidential Debates Inevitable?" *National Journal*, May 19, 1990, p. 1244.

5. Testimony of Hal Bruno, director of political coverage, ABC News, in *Presidential Debates*, hearings before the Subcommittee on Elections, p. 180.

6. "How He Won," *Newsweek*, special election issue, November/December 1992, pp. 83–85; Steven A. Holmes, "Movement on Debates Reflects Shifting Needs," *New York Times*, September 15, 1992, p. A23.

7. James Karayn, "The Case for Permanent Presidential Debates," in Austin Ranney, ed., *The Past and Future of Presidential Debates* (Washington, D.C.: American Enterprise Institute, 1979), p. 163.

8. Jim Karayn, "The Challenge of Presidential Debates," *Television Quarterly* 25, no. 4 (1992): 108.

9. Keith Darren Eisner, "Non-Major-Party Candidates and Televised Presidential Debates: The Merits of Legislative Inclusion," *University of Pennsylvania Law Review* 141, no. 3 (January 1993): 1018–19.

10. Representative Edward J. Markey in "National Presidential Debates Act of 1991," *Congressional Record*, February 26, 1991, p. E643.

11. Quoted by Edward J. Markey in ibid.

12. Quoted in Joel L. Swerdlow, *Beyond Debate: A Paper on Televised Presidential Debates* (New York: Twentieth Century Fund, 1984), p. 33.

13. Ibid.

14. Susan E. Spotts, "Recent Developments: The Presidential Debates Act of 1992," *Harvard Journal on Legislation* 29 (Summer 1992): 566.

15. Thomas H. Neale, *Campaign Debates in Presidential General Elections* (Washington, D.C.: Congressional Research Service, June 1993), p. 11.

16. See, among others, Eisner, "Non-Major-Party Candidates,"; Spotts, "Recent Developments: The Presidential Debates Act;" Scott M. Matheson, Jr., "Federal Legislation to Elevate and Enlighten Political Debate: A Letter and Report to the 102nd Congress about Constitutional Policy," *Journal of Law and Politics* 7, no. 1 (Fall 1990): 73–132.

17. Neale, *Campaign Debates in Presidential General Elections*, p. 12.

18. Testimony of Representative Al Swift in *Presidential Debates*, hearings before the Subcommittee on Elections, p. 2.

19. Testimony of Bobby Burchfield, general counsel of the Bush reelection committee, in ibid., pp. 53–54.

20. Markey, "National Presidential Debates Act of 1991," p. E643. See also Representative Timothy J. Penny, "The Democracy in Presidential Debates Act," *Congressional Record*, February 4, 1991, p. E397–98.

21. Neale, *Campaign Debates in Presidential General Elections*, p. 11.

22. See, among others, Spotts, "Recent Developments: The Presidential Debates Act," especially pp. 566–75.

23. See N.J. Stat. 19:44A–47 (1993) and N.J.S.A. 19:25–15.49 to 15.58.

24. Jerry Gray, "And Now, Whoppers vs. Waffles," *New York Times*, October 7, 1993, p. B8; Jerry Gray, "Rivals Wage Fierce Debate in New Jersey," *New York Times*, October 25, 1993, p. B1.

25. Matheson, "Federal Legislation to Elevate and Enlighten Political Debate," p. 118.

26. Testimony of Diana Carlin, associate professor of communication, University of Kansas, in *Presidential Debates*, hearings before the Subcommittee on Elections, p. 151.

27. Testimony of Kathleen Hall Jamieson, professor, Annenberg School for Communication, University of Pennsylvania, in ibid., p. 126.

28. Matheson, "Federal Legislation to Elevate and Enlighten Political Debate," p. 131.

29. Ibid.

30. Ibid., p. 132; testimony of Burchfield in *Presidential Debates*, hearings before the Subcommittee on Elections, pp. 56–58.

31. Testimony of Martin Plissner, political director, CBS News, in ibid., p. 112.

32. Sander Vanocur in Commission on Presidential Debates, "Review of 1992 Presidential Debates," p. 6.

33. See the statement of Arthur Block, special counsel to the New Alliance Party, in *Presidential Debates*, hearings before the Subcommittee on Elections, pp. 145–47.

34. See the statement of Stuart Reges, national director of the Libertarian Party, in ibid., especially pp. 165 and 169.

35. Eisner, "Non-Major-Party Candidates," pp. 1024–25.

36. For these arguments, see ibid.; see also the statements of Block and Reges in *Presidential Debates*, hearings before the Subcommittee on Elections.

37. Spotts, "Recent Developments: The Presidential Debates Act," p. 577.

38. See the comments of Warren Decker, director of the debate team, George Mason University, in *Presidential Debates*, hearings before the Subcommittee on Elections, p. 172.

39. Swerdlow, *Beyond Debate*, p. 37.

40. Ibid., p. 42.

41. Spotts, "Recent Developments: The Presidential Debates Act," p. 577; Eisner, "Non-Major-Party Candidates," p. 1020.

42. Under the provisions of the Federal Election Campaign Act, a candidate can qualify for federal matching funds in a presidential primary campaign by raising at least $5,000 in contributions of $250 or less in at least twenty states, for a total of $100,000. In 1992, three minor-party candidates—Lenora Fulani of the New Alliance Party, John Hagelin of the Natural Law Party, and Lyndon LaRouche—qualified for such funding. For a discussion of minor-party candidates and federal public financing programs, see

Anthony Corrado, *Paying for Presidents: Public Financing in National Elections* (New York: Twentieth Century Fund Press, 1993), pp. 45–48.

43. Frank Fahrenkopf, cochairman, Commission on Presidential Debates, in *Presidential Debates,* hearings before the Subcommittee on Elections, p. 82.

44. Testimony of Diana Carlin in ibid., p. 150.

45. Ibid.

46. Testimony of Kathleen Hall Jamieson in ibid., p. 105.

47. See *With the Nation Watching: Report of the Twentieth Century Fund Task Force on Televised Presidential Debates* (Lexington, Mass.: D. C. Heath and Company, 1979), p. 86; Swerdlow, *Beyond Debate,* p. 40.

48. Swerdlow, *Beyond Debate,* p. 40.

INDEX

ABOUT THE AUTHOR

A nthony Corrado is an Associate Professor of Government at Colby College in Waterville, Maine. He has had extensive practical experience in the management and financing of presidential campaigns as a member of the national staffs of the last three Democratic presidential nominees. In 1992, he served as national campaign coordinator of the Kerrey for President Committee and as a consultant for delegate and convention operations for the Clinton for President Committee. He is the author of *Creative Campaigning: PACs and the Presidential Selection Process* (Westview Press, 1992) and *Paying for Presidents* (Twentieth Century Fund Press, 1993), and coauthor of *Financing the 1992 Election* (M. E. Sharpe, 1995).